Little Knitted Garden Friends

15 Adorable Take-Along Pals to Create, Love, and Share

Val Pierce

Landauer Publishing

AF754551

32

38

44

50

56

62

68

74

80

86

92

98

Little Knitted
Garden Friends

Little Knitted Garden Friends

Landauer Publishing, *https://landauer.foxchapelpublishing.com*, is an imprint of Fox Chapel Publishing Company, Inc.

Copyright © 2026 by Val Pierce and Fox Chapel Publishing Company, Inc.

All rights reserved. No part of this book may be reproduced, stored in a retrieval system, or transmitted in any form or by any means, electronic, mechanical, photocopying, recording, or otherwise, without the prior written permission of Fox Chapel Publishing, except for the inclusion of brief quotations in an acknowledged review and the enlargement of the template patterns in this book for personal use only. The patterns themselves, however, are not to be duplicated for resale or distribution under any circumstances. Any such copying is a violation of copyright law.

Project Team
Editorial Director: Brian Hurley
Acquisitions Editor: Amelia Johanson
Technical Editor: Michael Harrigan
Editor: Christa Oestreich
Designer: Leslie Hall
Photographer: Steve Watts
Proofreader & Indexer: Gretchen Bacon

Shutterstock used: Art Kio (fabric background: back cover, 1, 2, 4–5, 128); giedre vaitekune (yarn balls: 3, 26); Touchr (bunting: 5); prapann (wooden sign: 5, 31, 32, 38, 44, 50, 56, 62, 68, 74, 80, 86, 92, 98, 104, 112, 118); LightField Studios (top left: 7); Ugorenkov Aleksandr (bottom left: 7); romiri (yarn ball: 8, 28); Melica (top, all: 9); PawelKacperek (yarn background: 32, 38, 44, 50, 56, 62, 68, 74, 80, 86, 92, 98, 104, 112, 118); New Africa (yarn ball: 41); ang intaravichian (yarn ball: 64); Liz Kcer (yarn ball: 82); AlinaMD (yarn ball: 109); c12 (yarn ball: 124).

ISBN 978-1-63981-167-0

Library of Congress Control Number: 2026935240

To learn more about the other great books from Fox Chapel Publishing, or to find a retailer near you, call toll-free at 800-457-9112 or visit us at www.FoxChapelPublishing.com.

We are always looking for talented authors.
To submit an idea, please send a brief inquiry to acquisitions@foxchapelpublishing.com.
Or write to:
Fox Chapel Publishing
903 Square Street
Mount Joy, PA 17552

MIX
Paper | Supporting responsible forestry
FSC® C016973

Printed in China
First printing

This book has been published with the intent to provide accurate and authoritative information in regard to the subject matter within. While every precaution has been taken in the preparation of this book, the author and publisher expressly disclaim any responsibility for any errors, omissions, or adverse effects arising from the use or application of the information contained herein.

Table of Contents

Introduction

Children love a knitted toy to play with, but toys can take quite a while to create and stitch together. Usually, they have numerous little pieces that, after completion, will need to be assembled. This can cause many issues: matching arms and legs, and making sure the head doesn't wobble on the body, not to mention stitching elaborate features that take ages to complete and look right.

With that in mind, I have created 15 sweet little characters, all of them just the right size for tiny hands—and best of all, they don't involve much in the way of stuffing and sewing up! These little friends are knitted all in one piece, then shaped after stuffing. There are no arms and legs to worry about and no head to stitch on, as these are all an integral part of the design. They take a very small amount of yarn, so they can be knitted from your stash in a day or a couple of evenings.

Once finished, they can be embellished as little or as much as your heart desires! I have included hats, scarves, bags, and even a little cape, which can be exchanged with most of the toys. Let your imagination run wild and customize the colors to suit your little one's tastes.

If you have never knitted a toy before, then these are a perfect place to start. Make one or make them all, and watch the child in your life have fun creating their own little world of magical garden friends! Even better—these easy but adorable little softies are perfect for donating to hospitals and children's charities.

Happy Knitting!

—Val

Getting Started

Before embarking on your project, it is wise to make sure that you have all the correct components on hand. It can be frustrating to have to stop and search for something or go out to buy what you need. I have therefore listed some recommendations for you in this section.

Supplies You'll Need

Yarn

- **YARN**—It can be quite daunting for a new knitter to decide which yarns to use for a project. The choices available these days are quite stunning and range from naturals to synthetics, alpaca, metallic, cashmere, silk, acrylic, and blends of wool, to name but a few. Remember to consider child and safety needs (page 11) when picking your yarn. For my knitted garden friends, I mostly used Stylecraft Special DK (100% Premium Acrylic; 322 yds [295m]; 3.5oz [100g]), which is a yarn that comes in a variety of pretty colors. I also used Stylecraft Life DK (72% Premium Acrylic, 25% Wool, 3% Vicose; 326 yds [298m]; 3.5oz [100g]) and King Cole Big Value Tweed DK (98% Premium Acrylic, 2% Vicose; 320 yds [293m]; 3.5oz [100g]) for a bit of interest.

- **EYELASH YARN**—This textured yarn has a feathery appearance that gives a fur to the Skunk and Squirrel designs. I used King Cole Moments DK (100% Polyester; 98 yds [90m]; 1.75oz [50g]), which is soft and snuggly—perfect for little ones. However, it is NOT for babies, as the fibers may shed.

- **KNITTING NEEDLES**—Knitting needles come in various lengths and many sizes. For our purposes, the projects in this book only require a US size 6 (4mm), US size 3 (3.25mm), and US size 5 (3.75mm) knitting needles.

- **STUFFING**—I find a quality brand of fiberfill polyester stuffing works very well, and it's what I use for all the toys in this book. As it's synthetic, fiberfill polyester is easy to wash and dry. This helps prevent dust mites and the growth of bacteria, making it especially good for children's toys.

Knitting Needles

Stuffing

Yarn Weight Guide

Here's a quick reference for the standard yarn weights. While the gauge and needle sizes are indicated here, these are just guidelines; each project indicates what I used.

Yarn Weight & Name	Type of Yarn	Gauge in Stockinette Stitch over 4" (10.2cm)	Recommended US Needle Size
LACE 0	Lace, 10-count crochet thread	33–40 sts*	000–1*
SUPER FINE 1	Sock, Fingering, Baby	27–32 sts	1–3
FINE 2	Sport, Baby	23–26 sts	3–5
LIGHT 3	DK, Light Worsted	21–24 sts	5–7
MEDIUM 4	Worsted, Afghan, Aran	16–20 sts	7–9
BULKY 5	Bulky, Chunky	12–15 sts	9–11
SUPER BULKY 6	Super Bulky, Roving	7–11 sts	11–17
JUMBO 7	Jumbo, Roving	6 sts or less	17 and larger

*Lace yarns are typically knit using larger needles to create loose, lacy patterns. Be sure to follow the recommendations for needle size and gauge included in your pattern.

Knitting Needle Guide

Here's a quick reference for the most common knitting needle sizes.

US Size	Millimeters	US Size	Millimeters
0	2mm	9	5.5mm
1	2.25mm	10	6mm
1.5	2.5mm	10.5	6.5mm
2	2.75mm	11	8mm
2.5	3mm	13	9mm
3	3.25mm	15	10mm
4	3.5mm	17	12mm
5	3.75mm	19	15mm
6	4mm	35	19mm
7	4.5mm	50	25mm
8	5mm	70	35mm

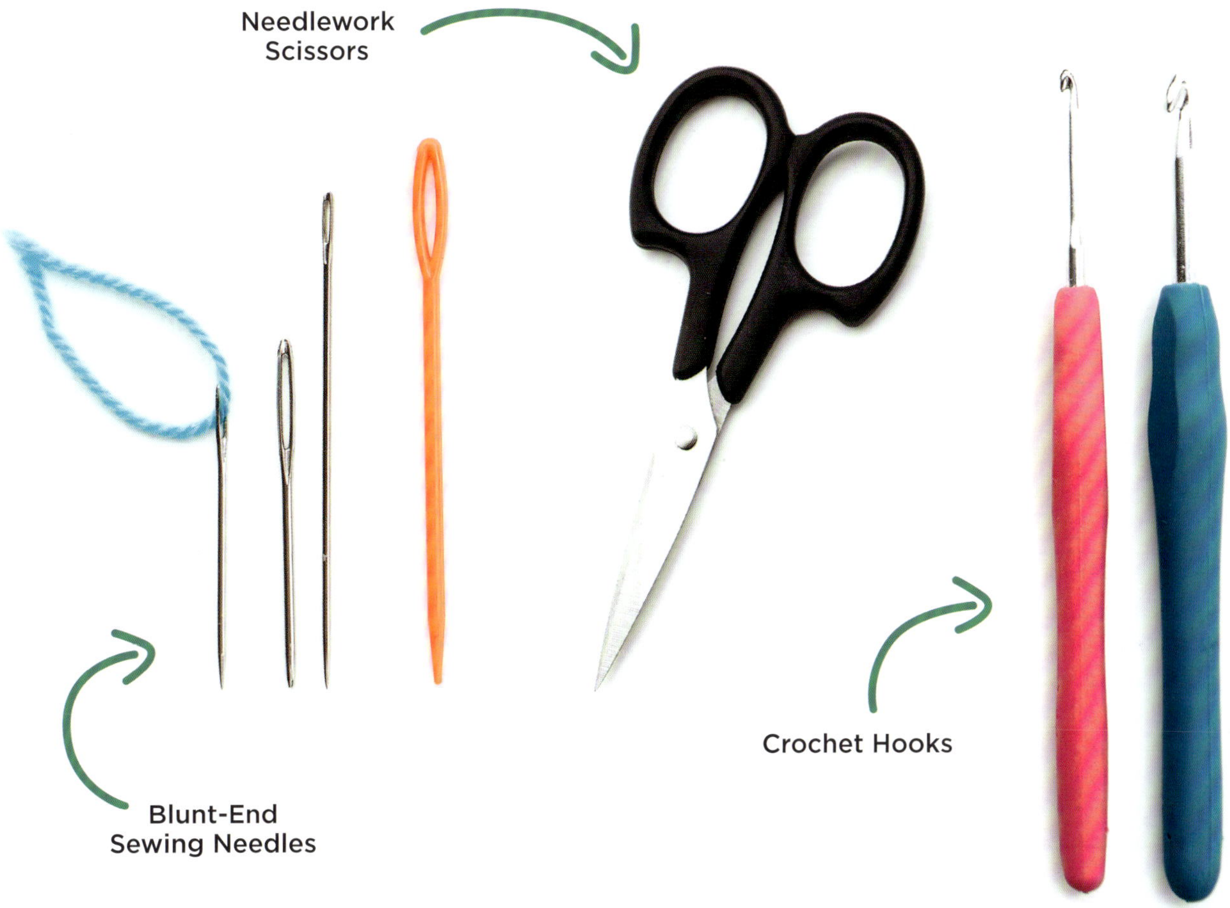

- **BLUNT-END SEWING NEEDLES**—For the duplicate stitch technique, which is used to add details to knitted fabric, it's best to use a blunt-end needle. This is to avoid splitting your knitting stitches.

- **CROCHET HOOK**—A large crochet hook is used to draw one piece through another to secure it in place, such as antennae on the Ladybug's hat.

- **NEEDLEWORK SCISSORS**—A sharp pair of needlework scissors should always be at hand for clipping your yarn.

- **SAFETY EYES**—You can opt to embroider the eyes on your softies, but if you'd like plastic eyes, make sure you select good-quality safety eyes. You want ones that will not release from your toy, as they could be choking hazards for younger children.

Hints and Tips

The basic stitches used in knitting the toys are explained in the Knitting Techniques section (page 13), so you can brush up on your knowledge if needed or even try your hand at learning to knit. The projects, however, are written for readers who have a good basic knowledge of the craft and aren't intended to teach you how to knit. (My previous book, *Learn to Knit the Easy Way*, will help you with that.)

The little garden friends are very easy to make; for the most part, they are knitted in just one piece. When sewn up, they form a tube that is then stuffed. The arms, legs, and head are defined by sewing through the knitted fabric. I have included a step-by-step tutorial (page 27) to guide you through making a basic toy prior to sharing individual patterns.

Some of the toys are a little more complex and have extra parts to knit separately, as well as a little color work, which adds simple patterns or accentuates faces. Features are added afterward. Any patternwork is very simple, and you will find extra instructions and charts in each of the patterns that contain these techniques.

Some of the toys have simple embroidery to enhance their features. These techniques will be explained with pictures and words in the Special Techniques section (page 24).

What is Gauge?

Count the rows in your gauge to determine if you should change needle sizes.

Gauge is very often overlooked and can have a detrimental effect on your finished piece. Correct tension determines the size of the piece you are knitting, so before embarking on a new project, it is imperative you make a sample swatch of at least 4" x 4" (10.2 x 10.2cm) using the number of stitches and rows stated in the instructions.

Always check your gauge before you begin working; if needed, change needle sizes to obtain the stated stitch count. If you get fewer stitches to the inch (centimeter) than stated, your gauge is too loose and a smaller needle is required. If you get more stitches to the inch (centimeter) than stated, your gauge is too tight and a larger needle is required. When measuring your gauge, don't stretch the work out or squish it up to make it fit; knit one or two samples until you get it just right.

Making Toys and Safety Issues

Keep materials in mind to make these toys both fun and safe to play with.

When making toys for children, safety is always paramount. As pretty as buttons and ribbons look, they are not sensible for play, especially when young children are the lucky recipients. I have outlined some of the most important things to consider before embarking on your chosen toy:

- **AGE**—Consider the age of the child the toy is intended for. When making toys, whatever their size, it's very important to bear in mind that children have very inquisitive hands and minds. The younger the child, the more care you need to take in your choices, such as the points below.
- **DURABILITY**—If you sew on any parts, then make sure they are very firm by overstitching each piece several times.
- **YARN**—Toys will need to be washed frequently, so a yarn and stuffing that are durable and easy to care for are sensible choices. Cotton is hard-wearing but tends to be less soft and fluffy than polyester. It can also clump after washings and is bit more expensive, but some may feel the cost is worth it for a special, handmade toy. Cotton is yarn is a good choice for babies, but it does tend to be quite expensive to buy and when knitted forms a firmer fabric. Acrylic yarns work equally well and are softer to the touch. Eyelash yarns or any yarns that could shed fibers are not recommended for babies. Cotton stuffing is also very good for children with allergies or skin sensitivities. However, polyester is less expensive and can feel softer and fluffier. It tends to stand the test of time a bit better than cotton fillings, as it's less likely to flatten.
- **CHOKING HAZARDS**—Wherever possible, embroider features onto the toy. If you decide to use safety eyes, which I've added to one or two of the animals in the book, then ensure you attach them correctly into the fabric—hearing a "click" sound when they are properly fastened. Don't add embellishments, buttons, or ribbons since they could come undone and pose a choking hazard.

Working from a Chart

Colored patterns and designs are often charted on graph paper, making them easy for the knitter to follow. Each square on the chart represents a stitch, and each horizontal line of squares represents a row of stitches. Charts can be either in color or black and white, using a key at the side with symbols to depict the different yarn colors used.

Charts are read from bottom to top and usually from right to left. They are usually in stockinette stitch, with odd-numbered rows being knit and even-numbered rows being purl. The first stitch of a chart is always at the bottom-right corner. Using a straightedge of some kind, like a ruler, under each row will help you keep your place in the chart as you work.

When working with more than one color, the best method of carrying yarn across a row is stranding (page 23).

Sewing Up and Stuffing

It's quite a simple process to sew up your little toy. To help you get started, there are photographs and step-by-step instructions for making a basic toy prior to the projects. Each toy is slightly different. Some have no arm and leg definition, but this will all be explained in the pattern instructions.

When stuffing your toy, take time to tease out small bits of the stuffing material for an even layer. Add a small amount at a time and shape the toy as you proceed. You need to get the amount just right for best effect. Under-stuffing will leave your little friend flat and lifeless, but overstuffing is equally as bad, as it can strain your stitches. As a guide, if you see the stuffing starting to show through your stitches, then you are overstuffing!

Knitting Techniques

The projects in this book all are fairly simple to make and use the basic stitches. To help you brush up on your knowledge, there are step-by-step instructions with photos to guide you through all the stitches used in the book. There are a few toys that use some more advanced techniques, so these are listed in a separate section.

Knitting Abbreviations

*	Repeat instructions between asterisks as indicated
**	Repeat instructions between double asterisks as indicated
()	Repeat instructions between parentheses as many times as indicated
"	Inch(es)
approx.	Approximately
beg	Beginning
CO	Cast on
cm	Centimeter(s)
g	Gram(s)
k	Knit
k2tog	Knit two stitches together, thus decreasing a stitch
k3tog	Knit three stitches together, thus decreasing two stitches
kfb	Knit into the front and back of the stitch
m1	Make a stitch by picking up the strand of yarn between the stitch you are working and the next stitch on the needle and knitting into the back of it, thus increasing one stitch
mm	Millimeter(s)
oz	Ounce(s)
p	Purl
p2tog	Purl two stitches together, thus decreasing a stitch
p3tog	Purl three stitches together, thus decreasing two stitches
psso	Pass slipped stitch over
rep	Repeat
SKP	Slip, knit, pass slipped stitch over
sl	Slip
st(s)	Stitch(es)
St st	Stockinette stitch
tbl	Through the back loop
tog	Together
yd(s)	Yard(s)
yo	Yarn over

Basic Techniques

CASTING ON

The first step in knitting is to learn to cast on. This forms the first row of stitches and one edge of the finished project, usually the bottom edge. There are many ways of casting on. Here are the two most used methods.

Two-Needle Method

Knitting begins with a foundation row of loops cast on to a needle. The other needle is used to build a series of interlocking loops in rows. Hold the needle with the stitches in your left hand and the needle to make the stitches in your right hand. (Left-handed people should work in reverse.)

Make a slip knot about 4" (10.2cm) from the end of the yarn and hold the needle in your left hand.

Insert the right-hand needle through the front loop and under the left-hand needle.

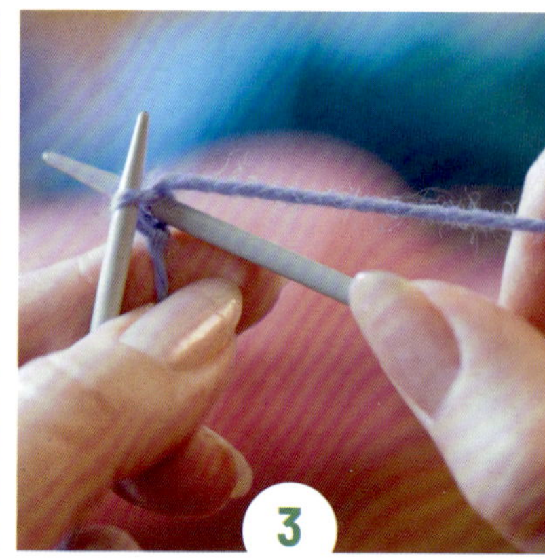

Pass the yarn under and over the point of the right-hand needle.

Using the right-hand needle, draw the yarn through the slip knot to form a stitch.

Transfer the new stitch onto the left-hand needle, placing it beside the slip knot. Insert the right-hand needle through the front of the new stitch and under the left-hand needle.

Take the working yarn under and over the point of the right-hand needle to form the next new stitch. Continue in this way until you have the stated number of stitches.

One-Needle or Thumb Method

This method gives a more elastic edge to the knitting.

1

Unwind sufficient yarn from the main ball to allow you to cast on the stated number of stitches. Wind the yarn twice around the thumb of your left hand.

2

Put the right-hand needle through the loop . . .

3

. . . and pull through to form a slip knot.

4

Hold the needle in your right hand, wind the yarn clockwise around your left thumb, and hold firmly.

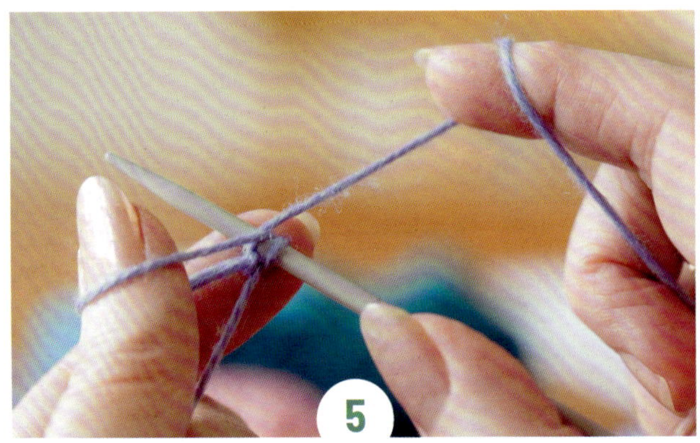

5

Insert the point of the needle through the loop, and wind the yarn in your left hand around the back of the point of the needle and in between the needle and your thumb. Pull the point of the needle under the thread, thus forming a stitch.

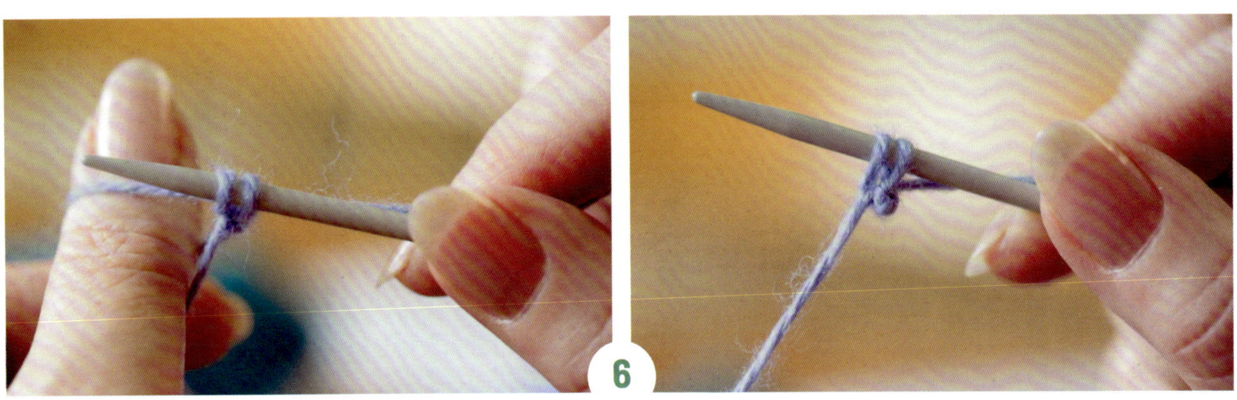

6

Slip the stitch onto the needle close to the slip knot. The first stitch is formed. Continue in this way until you have the stated number of stitches.

BINDING OFF

The technique of binding off is used to provide the finishing edge to the end of your work. It is also used when you need to shape pieces or to make buttonholes. You would usually bind off on the right side of the work; however, patterns will mostly tell you which side to do this.

When following some instructions, you will be told to bind off in the pattern that you are working, in order to give a particular finish. Don't pull the stitches too tightly when binding off, as this could result in a puckered edge or make it difficult when sewing up the garment or project.

Work the first two stitches in the pattern. **With the yarn at the back of the work, insert the point of the needle through the first stitch.

Lift the first stitch over the second stitch and then off the needle.

Work the next stitch in the pattern**. Now repeat the sequence from ** to ** until the stated number of stitches are bound off. You will be left with a single stitch at the end of the bind off; slip this off the needle and pull the end of the yarn through it quite firmly to secure.

KNIT STITCH

Now you can begin to form the first of two fundamental movements in knitting. The knit stitch forms a flat, vertical loop on the knitted fabric face. There are two widely used methods for forming this stitch, both of which are shown here.

Garter Stitch

Using just the knit stitch, you can create the garter stitch. It forms a firm, ridged fabric that is perfect for simple projects like headbands, scarves, and cushion covers.

English/American Method

In this method, use your right hand to pull the yarn around the right-hand needle. The amount of yarn used with each stitch is controlled by winding the working yarn in between your last two fingers. Your left hand moves the knitting forward while your right hand makes the stitch, lifting the yarn, placing it over the needle, and pulling it through the loop.

Holding the needle with the cast-on stitches in your left hand, wind the yarn around the little finger of your right hand, then under the next two fingers, and over the top of your forefinger.

Keeping the yarn at the back of the work, hold the second needle in your right hand and insert it into the front of the first stitch.

With your right forefinger, bring the yarn forward, moving under and over the point of the right-hand needle.

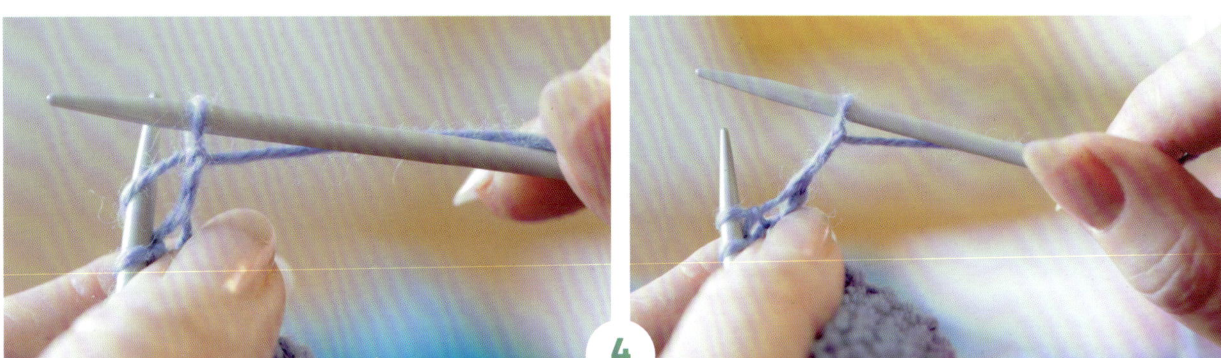

Pull the yarn through the loop and push the resulting stitch toward the point of the left-hand needle so that you can slip it onto the right-hand needle.

Continental Method

This method of knitting is often thought to be faster than holding the yarn in your right hand. Instead, you use the forefinger of your left hand to keep the yarn under tension and to pull the yarn onto the right-hand needle. The amount of yarn released, and therefore the tension, is controlled by the fingers. Raising your hand slightly will help keep the yarn taut.

Holding the needle with the cast-on stitches in your right hand, wind the yarn over your left forefinger and lay it across the palm of your hand. Take up the slack between your last two fingers.

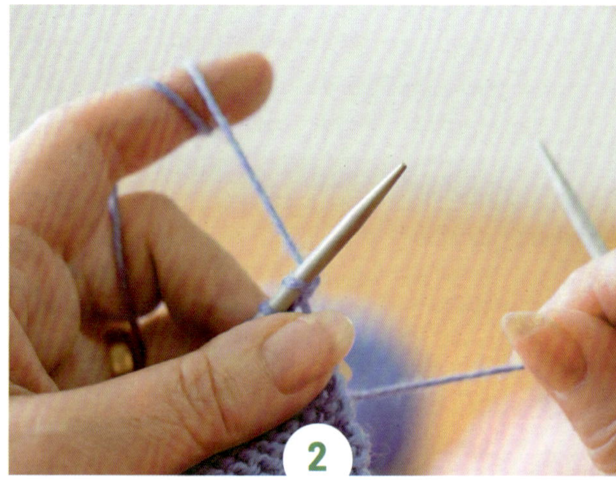

With the work in your left hand, extend your left forefinger, pulling the yarn behind the needle. Using your left thumb and middle finger, push the first stitch toward the point and insert the right-hand needle into the front of the stitch.

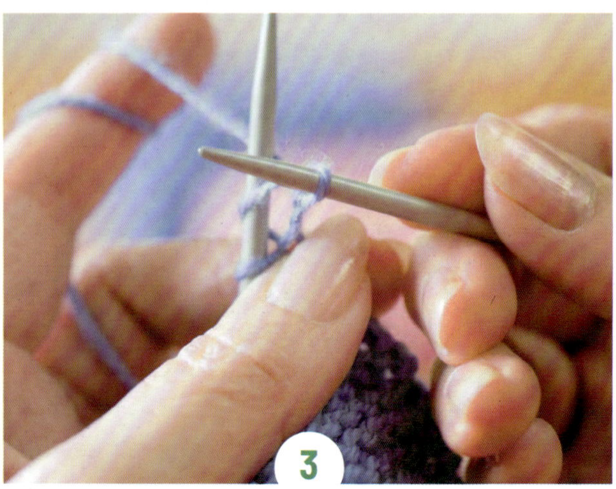

Twist the right-hand needle and place the right-hand point under the working yarn to pull the loop onto the right-hand needle.

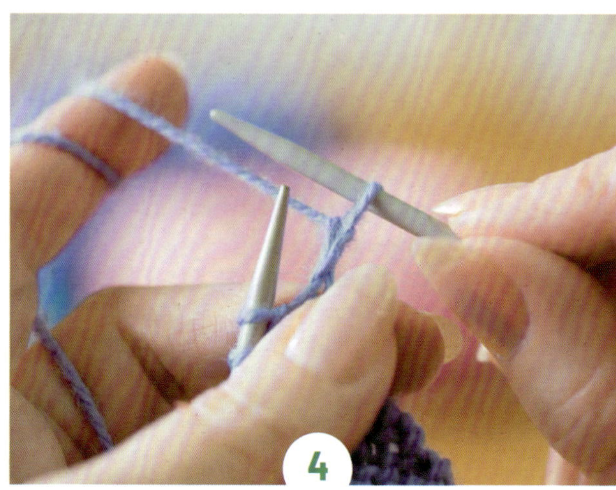

It may help to hold the loop with your right forefinger while you pull it down through the stitch. Pull the new stitch onto the right-hand needle.

PURL STITCH

The purl stitch is the other fundamental stitch used in knitting. Once you have learned and mastered these two techniques, the stitches will form the basis for a huge range of patterns. The two most widely used methods of forming the purl stitch are listed here.

English/American Method

With this method, the needle is put into the front of the stitch; then the yarn, which is held in the front, is wound over the back of the needle. Purl stitches sometimes tend to be a bit looser than knit ones, so keeping your fingers close to the work will help keep the stitches more even.

1

Holding the needle with either the cast-on or knit stitches in your left hand, wind the yarn around your little finger, under the next two fingers, and over the forefinger of your right hand.

2

With the yarn in the front of the work, pick up the needle in your right hand and insert the point into the front of the first stitch on the left-hand needle.

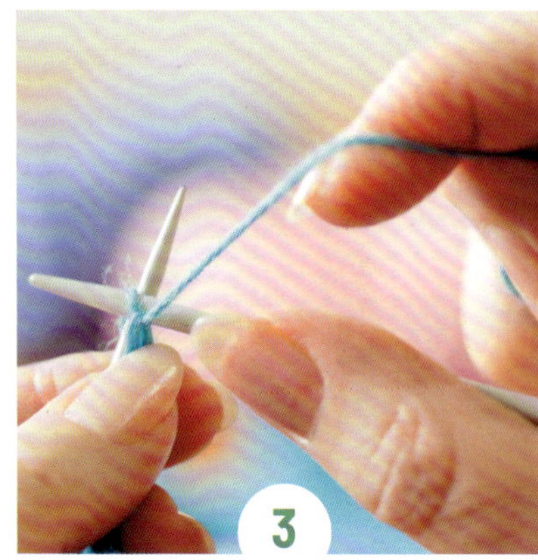

3

With your right-hand forefinger, wind the yarn over the point of the right-hand needle and then under it.

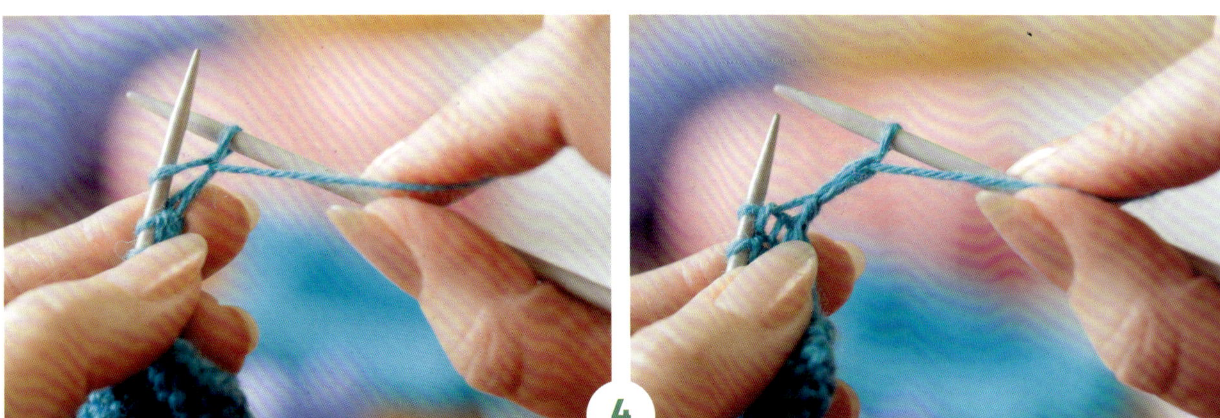

4

Pull the loop on the right-hand needle through the stitch and push the new stitch toward the point of the left-hand needle. You are now able to slip the stitch off the right-hand needle.

Continental Method

When using this method, your left forefinger holds the working yarn tight while you pick up the new loop with the right-hand needle. This movement is helped by twisting your left wrist forward to release the yarn. Then, using your middle finger, push the yarn toward the point of the needle.

Holding the needle with the stitches in your right hand, take the yarn over your left forefinger, lay it across your palm, and take up the slack between your last two fingers.

Holding the work in your left hand, push out your left forefinger slightly, pulling the working yarn in front of the needle. Using your left thumb and middle finger, push the first stitch toward the point and insert the right-hand needle into the front of the stitch. Hold the stitch with your right forefinger.

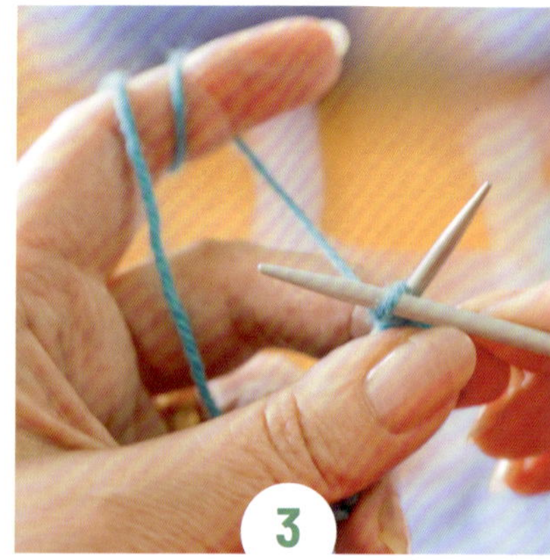

Twist your left wrist back slightly, then use the forefinger of your left hand to wind the yarn around the right-hand needle.

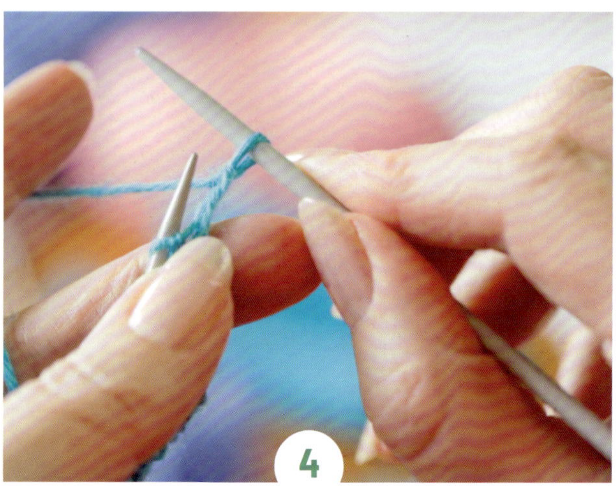

Push down and back with the right-hand needle to pull the loop through the stitch . . .

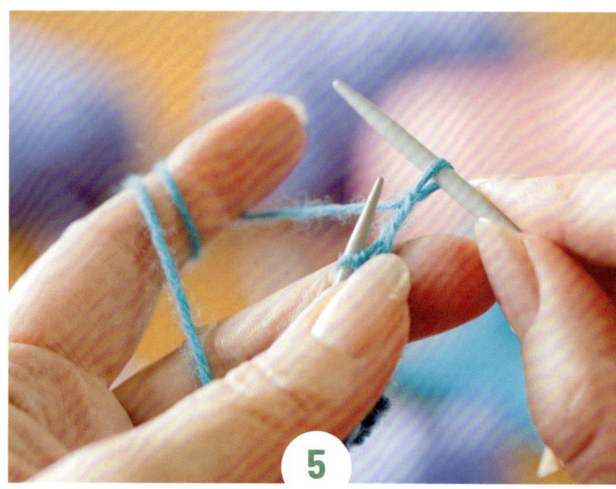

. . . and slip the new stitch onto the right-hand needle. Straighten out your left forefinger to tighten the new stitch and control the tension.

STOCKINETTE STITCH

The stockinette stitch is one of the easiest and most versatile stitches to master when learning to knit. It is formed by working two rows alternately. On the first row, you will knit all the stitches; on the second, you will purl all the stitches. These two rows are then repeated.

We are using straight needles to knit this sample, which produce a smooth, even fabric that is not reversible. The fabric is quite stretchy, has excellent drape, and is mostly used for wearable garments like hats, sweaters, scarves, and mittens.

Stockinette-stitch fabric does tend to curl as you knit it. The top and bottom edges curl inward to the right side of your work while the side edges curl toward the wrong side of the work. You are not doing anything wrong here—it happens to every knitter! There are ways to counteract this tendency, such as working border stitches in garter stitch (page 17).

Remember

- When working the **KNIT ROW**, the yarn should be at the **BACK** of your work.
- When working the **PURL ROW**, the yarn should be at the **FRONT** of your work.

When you first knit the stockinette stitch, you may find that the fabric isn't as even as you would like. This is usually because the stitches on one of the rows are slightly tighter than on the others. The knit row always seems easier to master than the purl row. Practice will normally ensure an even, smooth result.

Knit Row

The knit row, which is the first row you will knit, is most always termed the right side of your work. The appearance and feel of the fabric are quite smooth. When you look closely, you will see vertical rows of tiny V shapes that form the stitches.

Purl Row

This side is often called the wrong side. Sometimes you will need to count rows as you work, and it's much easier to get an accurate count if you count on the purl side of your work. The purl row will produce rows of tiny bumps and is less smooth to the touch. It's quite easy to see the rows, as they form horizontal ridges.

KNITTING WITH MORE THAN ONE COLOR

There are many ways of enhancing your knitting with the use of color. Nowadays, there is a fantastic array of colored and textured yarns available that will make your choice a very exciting one. One of the simplest ways to add color to is to make horizontal stripes, joining in new shades of yarn at the beginnings of rows. Combining different-textured yarns can also produce stunning effects on knitwear, but care must be taken to make sure the yarns are of a similar weight or the tension produced will vary too much and may spoil your piece. Other ways to incorporate color include block knitting, which entails using separate balls of yarn for each color and then twisting the yarns together at the back of the work when changing colors to avoid making holes. Intarsia is another method and entails the need to use separate balls of yarn for each colored stitch represented on a chart.

Adding at the Start of a Row

Use this method when working horizontal stripes.

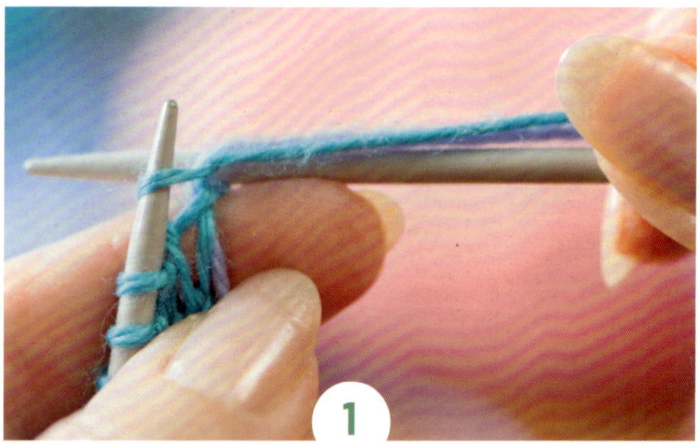

Insert the right-hand needle into the first stitch on the left-hand needle and wind both the old and new yarns over it. Knit the stitch with both yarns.

Drop the old yarn and pick up the new yarn. Knit the next two stitches with the short end and the working yarn.

Drop the short end of the new yarn and continue knitting in pattern. On the subsequent row, purl the three double stitches in the normal way.

Adding Within the Row

Follow this method when using the original yarn again in the same row. The yarn not in use has to be carried along the back of the work. Use stranding (see below) when there are just a few stitches that need to be knitted in a different color (not more than four or five stitches). Failure to do this will leave long strands of yarn at the back of the work, which will spoil the knitted fabric.

With the old yarn at the back of the work, insert the point of the right-hand needle into the stitch. Wind the new yarn over the needle and use it as your new stitch.

Knit the next two stitches with both the new and old colors.

Drop the short end and continue knitting with the new yarn while carrying the old yarn across the back. On subsequent rows, purl the double stitches normally.

Stranding

When using more than one color in a row, the yarn—which is sometimes known as a float—is picked up and carried across the back of the work to make the next new stitch. This yarn should be carried across the back of the work at the same tension as your knitting. If you pull it too tightly, it will pucker the work; if it is left too loose, the work will have holes or larger stitches where the different colors were changed. Much practice is needed to perfect this technique.

Special Techniques

MATTRESS STITCH

This method of joining your knitted pieces together works well on thicker fabric. Have the right sides of the pieces facing you as you sew to make it easier to align the rows, especially when joining stripes or patterns. The seam that is formed is almost invisible on the right side and has a narrow ridge on the wrong side of the work.

1 Secure the yarn at the base of the pieces. Insert the blunt-end needle into the horizontal strand of the stitch on the right-hand side of the fabric.

2 Pull the yarn through the stitch.

3 Insert the blunt-end needle into the horizontal strand of the corresponding stitch on the left-hand side of the fabric.

4 Pull the yarn through the stitch.

5 Continue in this way, repeating steps 1–4 until your seam is complete. Even out the stitches to form the neat, almost invisible seam.

DUPLICATE STITCH

This technique is used to add detail to knitted fabric, specifically on stockinette stitch projects. It's a very versatile technique since it allows you to add decorative elements to your finished projects after they are completed by stitching over the existing knit stitch. It's perfect for adding a few contrast stitches onto areas, such as some of the little toys in this book.

The duplicate stitch takes a little time and practice to master, as is the case with every new technique. The secret is to always use a blunt-end needle; this prevents splitting stitches/strands as you work. Do not pull the yarn too tightly or it will spoil the finish, causing the underneath stitch to show through.

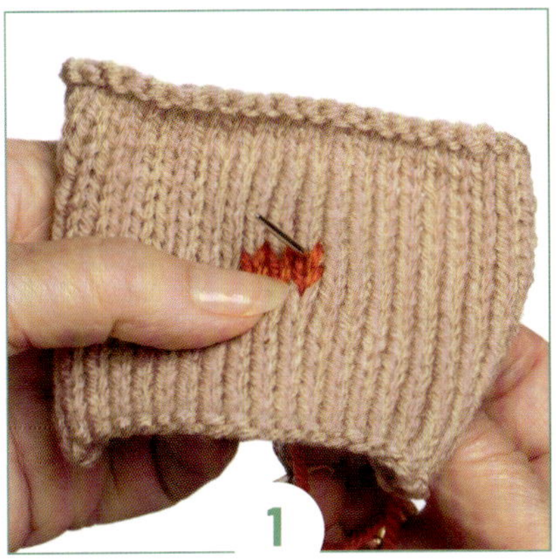

From the back of the work, bring the blunt-end needle through the center of the base of the V stitch you want to cover. Pull yarn through to the right side of the work.

Insert the needle through the two strands at the top of the V.

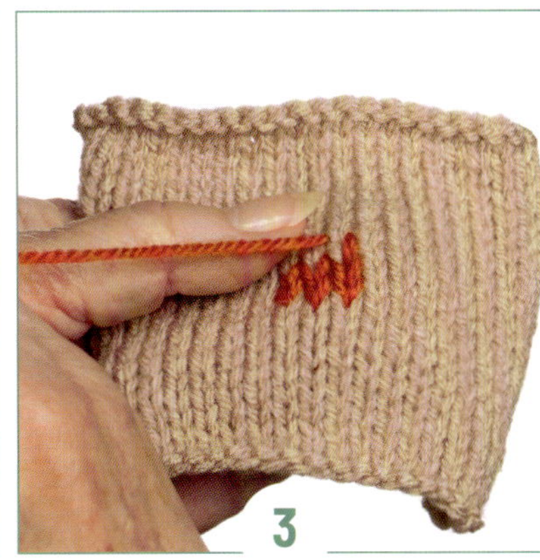

Pull yarn through, thus covering the right-hand side of the V.

Insert the needle back into the base of the V.

Pull the stitch through to the back of the work, thus completing the stitch.

CHAIN STITCH

Another stitch that I have used in the book is a very simple embroidery stitch, called chain stitch. This is an easy one to learn and use, as it is made with just a few steps. The chains made link with each other and can be used to outline—as they are in this book—to fill in, to add curves, or to accentuate colors.

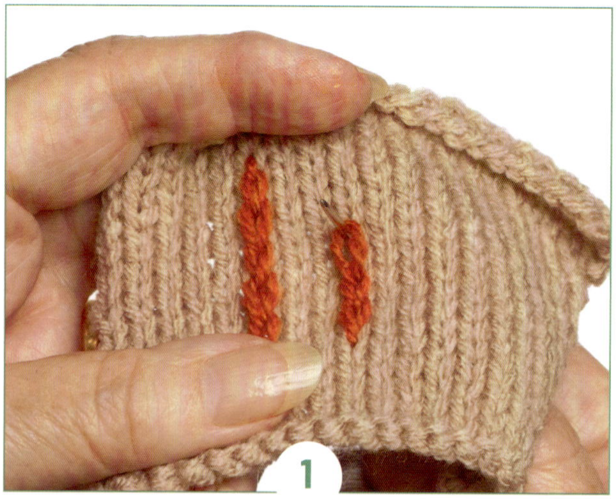

1

Bring the blunt-end needle from the back of the work where you want the chain to start. If you've already done a chain, bring the needle through the top of the previous chain loop.

2

Pull the yarn through. Hold the yarn firmly with your finger and begin to form a loop.

3

Push the needle back through the fabric from the front, at the same point where you started, to form the chain.

Repeat steps 1–3 to form consecutive chains. When you have worked the desired amount, bind off the yarn at the back of the work.

4

Step-by-Step Basic Toy

Assembling the little garden friends is quite a simple process. To make it clear, I am going to show you with some step-by-step instructions and photos. We are going to work on the Bunny (page 32) here, but the other animals are all made in a similar way. Any variations for other animals are explained in the pattern instructions.

Following the pattern instructions, knit the basic shape, which will look like an oblong. Gather the top of the piece to form the head.

Fold the piece so the seam runs down the center back. Sew the edges together using the mattress stitch, matching any stripes or patterning.

Stuff the piece, teasing out the stuffing as you do. This will achieve a smooth finish for the toy. Shape the head until it is nicely rounded. Do not overstuff.

With a blunt-end needle and matching yarn, form the head by stitching around the marked neck row. Insert a blunt-end needle at the right-hand side of the back seam and secure it with a few stitches. Run the needle through each stitch all around the row.

Draw up quite firmly to form the head. Add or remove some stuffing as you do to get the correct shape. Secure at the back of the toy.

Gather the base of the toy. Proceed to stitch vertically through both thicknesses of fabric to form the legs.

To sew the arms, turn the toy sideways, count 8 sts horizontally from the center-back join, and mark this point. Count 8 rows from the marked point and add another marker. These center 8 rows form the arm seam. Sew a line vertically through the fabric. Repeat on the other side for the second arm.

Following the pattern instructions, make the ears. For ears that are wider at the middle than the base, pinch them together at the base and sew through the stitch at either end to achieve the pointed shape.

Repeat with the second ear. Sew both ears to the top of the toy's head.

Using a blunt-end needle and contrasting yarn, embroider the eyes onto the face by making several diagonal or vertical stitches. Optionally, make one stitch for the eyebrow.

Using a blunt-end needle and yarn in the indicated color, embroider the nose by making a few horizontal stitches.

We have our completed bunny!

Projects

It's time to start knitting our little friends. Pick your favorite or start with the Bunny and work to the Squirrel in order of difficulty. They're the perfect little hand-sized pets to make and gift to your loved ones or donate to child-focused charities.

Basil the Bunny

This adorable bunny wears a satchel that gives little ones a secret hiding place for their tiny treasures. I've dressed him in a spring green sweater, but you can choose whatever color is your favorite.

If you love bunnies in your garden but prefer they don't nibble on all your plants, mix in some lavender and snapdragons, which they don't find appealing.

Height:

8" (20.3cm) measured from the tip of the ears to the base of the legs

Materials:

- DK weight (#3 light) yarn, approx. 1 oz (28.3g) in each shade:
  - **Color A** = Parchment (1218)
  - **Color B** = Cypress (1824)
  - **Color C** = Black (1002)
  - **Color D** = Candyfloss (1130)
  - **Color E** = Pistachio (1822)
- US size 6 (4mm) and US size 3 (3.25mm) knitting needles, or sizes required for gauge
- Blunt-end sewing needle
- Needlework scissors
- Stuffing

Gauge:

- 22 sts x 30 rows measure 4" x 4" (10.2 x 10.2cm) using US size 6 (4mm) needles and stockinette stitch.
- 24 sts x 36 rows measure 4" x 4" (10.2 x 10.2cm) using US size 3 (3.25mm) needles and stockinette stitch.

Pattern Notes:

- The main piece of the bunny is made in one piece. The ears and bag are made separately.

Special Safety Note

The tiny carrots shown are for display purposes only to enhance the photograph and would be a safety hazard for little ones.

BODY

Begin at the base of the legs.

Using Color A and US size 6 (4mm) needles, CO 34 sts.

Rows 1–12: Work in St st.

Break Color A.

Sweater

Continuing from the body, join Color B.

Rows 1–2: Knit all stitches.

Row 3: Purl all stitches.

Rows 4–5: Knit all stitches.

Row 6: Purl all stitches.

Rows 7–8: Knit all stitches.

Rows 9–20: Rep Rows 5–8.

Rows 21–22: Rep Rows 5–6.

Break Color B.

Head

Continuing from the sweater, join Color A.

Rows 1–12: Work in St st.

The next row starts shaping the head:

Row 13: *K2, k2tog*, rep from * to * to the last 2 sts, k2. (26 sts)

Row 14: Purl all stitches.

Row 15: *K1, k2tog*, rep from * to * to the last 2 sts, k2. (18 sts)

Row 16: Purl all stitches.

Row 17: K2tog to the end. (9 sts)

Row 18: Purl all stitches.

Break yarn and run through sts on the needle. Draw up tightly and bind off.

EARS (MAKE 2)

Using Color A and US size 3 (3.25mm) needles, CO 3 sts.

Row 1: Knit all stitches.

Row 2: Kfb, k1, kfb. (5 sts)

Row 3: Knit all stitches.

Row 4: Kfb, k3, kfb. (7 sts)

Row 5: Knit all stitches.

Row 6: Kfb, k5, kfb. (9 sts)

Rows 7–17: Knit all stitches.

Row 18: K2tog, k5, k2tog. (7 sts)

Row 19: Knit all stitches.

Row 20: K2tog, k3, k2tog. (5 sts)

Row 21: Knit all stitches.

Row 22: K2tog, k1, k2tog. (3 sts)

Row 23: K3tog.

Bind off.

SHOULDER BAG

Using Color E and US size 3 (3.25mm) needles, CO 9 sts.

Rows 1–22: Knit all stitches.

Row 23: K2tog, knit to the last 2 sts, k2tog. (7 sts)

Row 24: Knit all stitches.

Row 25: K2tog, k3, k2tog. (5 sts)

Row 26: K2tog, k1, k2tog. (3 sts)

Row 27: K3tog.

Bind off.

BAG STRAP

Using Color E and US size 3 (3.25mm) needles, CO 3 sts.

Rows 1–50: Knit all stitches.

Bind off.

ASSEMBLING THE TOY

Follow the Step-by-Step Basic Toy instructions (page 27) for sewing the animal together, stuffing quite firmly as you do. Shape the head into a nice rounded shape after gathering at the neckline. Embroider the eyes and eyebrows using Color C, and embroider the nose with Color D. Pin an ear i place onto the head. Pleat the base a little to give ear shape, then sew firmly in place. Repeat with tl other ear.

Fold the shoulder bag in half, overlapping the pointed end to form the flap. Sew the side seams using the mattress stitch, leaving the top of the bag open. Sew the bag strap to either side of the shoulder bag. Place around the animal's neck to hang down one side.

Haddie the Hedgehog

Our hedgehog is prepared for a little garden frost in his matching scarf and hat.

Did you know that hedgehogs are critical to maintaining a garden's ecosystem by eating insects and controlling the pest population?

Height:

7" (17.8cm) measured from the top of the head to the base of the legs

Materials:

- DK weight (#3 light) yarn, approx. 1 oz (28.3g) in each shade:

  Color A = Sandstone (1126)

  Color B = Cream (1005)

  Color C = Cinder Rose (2171)

  Color D = Black (1002)

  Color E = Toy (1844)
- US size 6 (4mm) knitting needles, or size required for gauge
- Blunt-end sewing needle
- Needlework scissors
- Stuffing

Gauge:

- 22 sts x 30 rows measure 4" x 4" (10.2 x 10.2cm) using US size 6 (4mm) needles and stockinette stitch.

Pattern Notes:

- The main piece of the hedgehog is made in one piece. The head cover, hat, and scarf are made separately.

BODY

Begin at the base of the legs.

Using Color A, CO 34 sts.

Rows 1–2: Knit all stitches.

Wind two small balls, one each of Colors A and B. Twist the yarns together when changing colors to ensure there are no holes in the work.

Row 3: Using A, (k1, p1) 5 times, k1; using B, k12; using A, (k1, p1) 5 times, k1.

Row 4: K11 A, p12 B, k11 A.

Rows 5–32: Rep Rows 3–4.

Break Colors A and B.

Head

Continuing from the body, join Color E.

Rows 1–12: Work in St st.

The next row starts shaping the head:

Row 13: *K2, k2tog*, rep from * to * to the last 2 sts, k2. (26 sts)

Row 14: Purl all stitches.

Row 15: *K1, k2tog*, rep from * to * to the last 2 sts, k2. (18 sts)

Row 16: Purl all stitches.

Row 17: K2tog to the end. (9 sts)

Row 18: Purl all stitches.

Break yarn and run through sts on the needle. Draw up tightly and bind off.

HEAD COVER

Using Color A, CO 2 sts.

Row 1: Knit all stitches.

Row 2: (Kfb) 2 times. (4 sts)

Row 3: Knit all stitches.

Row 4: Kfb, k2, kfb. (6 sts)

Row 5: Knit all stitches.

Row 6: Kfb, k4, kfb. (8 sts)

Row 7: Knit all stitches.

Row 8: CO 2 sts, knit to the end. (10 sts)

Row 9: Rep Row 9. (12 sts)

Row 10: Knit all stitches.

Row 11: Kfb at each end of the row. (14 sts)

Row 12: Rep Row 12. (16 sts)

Row 13: CO 4 sts, knit to end. (20 sts)

Row 14: Rep Row 14. (24 sts)

Row 15: Kfb at each end. (26 sts)

Row 16: *K1, p1*, repeat from * to * to end.

Row 17: Knit all stitches.

Rows 18–29: Rep Rows 17–18.

Row 30: *K4, k2tog*, rep from * to * to the last 2 sts, k2. (22 sts)

Row 31: Knit all stitches.

Row 32: *K1, k2tog*, rep from * to * to the last st, k1. (16 sts)

Row 33: Knit all stitches.

Row 34: K2tog to the end. (8 sts)

Break yarn and run through sts on the needle. Draw up tightly and bind off.

SCARF

Using Color C, CO 3 sts.

Row 1: Knit all stitches.

Row 2: Kfb, k1, kfb. (5 sts)

Row 3: Knit all stitches.

Row 4: Kfb, k3, kfb. (7 sts)

Rows 5–22: Knit all stitches.

Row 23: K2tog, knit to the last 2 sts, k2tog. (5 sts)

Row 24: Knit all stitches.

Row 25: K2tog, knit to the last 2 sts, k2tog. (3 sts)

Rows 26–62: Knit all stitches.

Row 63: Kfb, k1, kfb. (5 sts)

Row 64: Knit all stitches.

Row 65: Kfb, k3, kfb. (7 sts)

Rows 66–84: Knit all stitches.

Row 85: K2tog, knit to the last 2 sts, k2tog. (5 sts)

Row 86: Knit all stitches.

Row 87: K2tog, knit to the last 2 sts, k2tog. (3 sts)

Bind off.

WINTER HAT

Using Color C, CO 34 sts.

Row 1: K2, *p2, k2*, rep from * to * to the end.

Row 2: P2, *k2, p2*, rep from * to * to the end.

Rows 3–4: Rep Rows 1-2.

Rows 5–12: Work in garter stitch (knit every row).

Row 13: *K2, k2tog*, rep from * to * to the last 2 sts, k2. (26 sts)

Row 14: Knit all stitches.

Row 15: *K1, k2tog*, rep from * to * to the last 2 sts, k2. (18 sts)

Row 16: Knit all stitches.

Row 17: K2tog to the end. (9 sts)

Row 18: Knit all stitches.

Break yarn and run through sts on the needle. Draw up tightly and bind off.

ASSEMBLING THE TOY

Follow the Step-by-Step Basic Toy instructions (page 27) for sewing the animal together, stuffing quite firmly as you do. Shape the head into a nice, rounded shape after gathering at the neckline. Embroider the eyes and nose with Color D.

Pin the pointed end of the head cover onto the front of the head, just above the nose. Pull the cover over the head and secure at the back of the neck. Shape the front around the eyes and the sides of the head. Use the pictures as a guide if needed. Sew in place onto the head.

Wrap the scarf around the neck. Sew the seam on the winter hat using the mattress stitch. Place at an angle on the head.

Darcey the Snowy Deer

Our deer is quite the handsome buck in his stockinette sweater. While most folks go out of their way to keep deer out of their yards, who can't help but welcome this fun fellow into theirs?

Height:

7 ½" (19.1cm) measured from the tip of the antlers to the base of the legs

Materials:

- DK weight (#3 light) yarn, approx. 1 oz (28.3g) in each shade:
  - **Color A** = Vintage Peach (1836)
  - **Color B** = Parchment (1218)
  - **Color C** = Walnut (1054)
  - **Color D** = Cream (1005)
  - **Color E** = Black (1002)
- US size 6 (4mm) knitting needles, or size required for gauge
- Blunt-end sewing needle
- Needlework scissors
- Stuffing

Gauge:

- 22 sts x 30 rows measure 4" x 4" (10.2 x 10.2cm) using US size 6 (4mm) needles and stockinette stitch.

Pattern Notes:

- The main piece of the deer is made in one piece. The ears and antlers are made separately.

BODY

Begin at the base of the legs.

Using Color C, CO 34 sts.

Rows 1–2: Work in St st.

Break Color C and join Color B.

Rows 3–12: Work in St st.

Break Color C.

Sweater

Continuing from the body, join Color A.

Rows 1–4: Knit all stitches.

Begin pattern:

Row 5: * K2, p2*, rep from * to * to the last 2 sts, k2.

Row 6: * P2, k2*, rep from * to * to the last 2 sts, p2.

Row 7: *P2, k2*, rep from * to * to the last 2 sts, p2.

Row 8: *K2, p2*, rep from * to * to the last 2 sts, k2.

Rows 9–16: Rep Rows 5–8.

Rows 17–18: Rep Rows 5–6.

Rows 19–20: Knit all stitches.

Break Color A.

Head

Continuing from the sweater, join Color D.

Rows 1–6: Work in St st.

Break Color D and join Color B.

Rows 7–12: Work in St st.

The next row starts shaping the head:

Row 13: *K2, k2tog*, rep from * to * to the last 2 sts, k2. (26 sts)

Row 14: Purl all stitches.

Row 15: *K1, k2tog*, rep from * to * to the last 2 sts, k2. (18 sts)

Row 16: Purl all stitches.

Row 17: K2tog to the end. (9 sts)

Row 18: Purl all stitches.

Break yarn and run through sts on the needle. Draw up tightly and bind off.

EARS (MAKE 2)

Using Color B, CO 3 sts.

Row 1: Knit all stitches.

Row 2: Kfb, k1, kfb. (5 sts)

Row 3: Knit all stitches.

Row 4: Kfb, k3, kfb. (7 sts)

Row 5: Knit all stitches.

Row 6: K2tog, k3, k2tog. (5 sts)

Row 7: Knit all stitches.

Row 8: K2tog, k1, k2tog. (3 sts)

Row 9: Knit all stitches.

Row 10: K3tog.

Bind off.

ANTLERS (MAKE 2)

Using Color C, CO 20 sts.

Rows 1–3: Work in St st.

Bind off.

ASSEMBLING THE TOY

Follow the Step-by-Step Basic Toy instructions (page 27) for sewing the animal together, stuffing quite firmly as you do. Shape the head into a nice, rounded shape after gathering at the neckline. Embroider the eyes and nose using Color E. Pin an ear in place onto the head. Pleat the base a little to give the ear shape, then sew firmly in place. Repeat with the other ear.

Mark 11 sts along one antler strip; fold together at this point to form one long and one short tine. Sew together along 5 sts from the point of the fold using the mattress stitch. Make the other antler in the same way. Sew the antlers to the top of the head between the ears.

Using a blunt-end needle and Color C, work three duplicate stitches onto the center of the head in random places. Refer to the photographs for guidance if needed.

Barnaby the Bear

Some of us wouldn't expect to find a bear roaming around in our gardens—unless, of course, that garden happens to be near the mountains. However, a collection of animal softies wouldn't be complete without a teddy bear friend. Ours is smartly dressed in a purple knit-stitch cardigan.

Height:

6 ½" (16.5cm) measured from the tip of the ears to the base of the legs

Materials:

- DK weight (#3 light) yarn, approx. 1 oz (28.3g) in each shade:
  - **Color A** = Dark Brown (1004)
  - **Color B** = Magenta (1084)
  - **Color C** = Black (1002)
  - **Color D** = Stone (1710)
- US size 6 (4mm) and US size 3 (3.25mm) knitting needles, or sizes required for gauge
- Blunt-end sewing needle
- Needlework scissors
- Stuffing

Gauge:

- 22 sts x 30 rows measure 4" x 4" (10.2 x 10.2cm) using US size 6 (4mm) needles and stockinette stitch.
- 24 sts x 36 rows measure 4" x 4" (10.2 x 10.2cm) using US size 3 (3.25mm) needles and stockinette stitch.

Pattern Notes:

- The main piece of the bear is made in one piece. The ears and muzzle are made separately.
- Chain stitch outlines the neck and front band of the cardigan.

BODY

Begin at the base of the legs.

Using Color A and US size 6 (4mm) needles, CO 34 sts.

Rows 1–12: Work in St st.

Break Color A.

Cardigan

Continuing from the body, join Color B.

Rows 1–4: Knit all stitches.

Row 5: *K1, p1*, rep from * to * to the end.

Row 6: * P1, k1*, rep from * to * to the end.

Rows 7–14: Rep Rows 5–6.

Wind two small balls, one each of Colors A and B. Twist the yarns together when changing colors to ensure there are no holes in the work.

Row 15: Using B, (k1, p1) 8 times; k2 A; using B, (k1, p1) 8 times.

Row 16: Using B, (p1, k1) 7 times, p1; p4 A; using B, (k1, p1) 7 times, k1.

Row 17: Using B, (k1, p1) 7 times; k6 A; using B, (k1, p1) 7 times.

Row 18: Using B, (p1, k1) 6 times, p1; p8 A; using B, (k1, p1) 6 times, k1.

Row 19: Using B, (k1, p1) 6 times; k10 A; using B, (k1, p1) 6 times.

Row 20: Using B, (p1, k1) 6 times; p10 A; using B, (p1, k1) 6 times.

Break Color B.

Head

Continuing from the cardigan, work in Color A only.

Rows 1–12: Work in St st.

The next row starts shaping the head:

Row 13: *K2, k2tog*, rep from * to * to the last 2 sts, k2. (26 sts)

Row 14: Purl all stitches.

Row 15: *K1, k2tog*, rep from * to * to the last 2 sts, k2. (18 sts)

Row 16: Purl all stitches.

Row 17: K2tog to the end. (9 sts)

Row 18: Purl all stitches.

Break yarn and run through sts on the needle. Draw up tightly and bind off.

MUZZLE

Using Color D and US size 3 (3.25mm) needles, CO 3 sts.

Rows 1–2: Knit all stitches.

Row 3: Kfb, k1, kfb. (5 sts)

Row 4: Knit all stitches.

Row 5: Kfb, k3, kfb. (7 sts)

Row 6: Knit all stitches.

Row 7: K2tog, knit to the last 2 sts, k2tog. (5 sts)

Row 8: Knit all stitches.

Row 9: K2tog, k1, k2tog. (3 sts)

Row 10: Knit all stitches.

Bind off.

EARS (MAKE 2)

Using Color A and US size 3 (3.25mm) needles, CO 3 sts.

Row 1: Knit all stitches.

Row 2: Kfb to the end. (6 sts)

Row 3: Kfb, k4, kfb. (8 sts)

Rows 4–5: Knit all stitches.

Row 6: (K2tog) 4 times. (4 sts)

Bind off.

ASSEMBLING THE TOY

Follow the Step-by-Step Basic Toy instructions (page 27) for sewing the animal together, stuffing quite firmly as you do. Shape the head into a nice, rounded shape after gathering at the neckline. Pin an ear in place onto the head, curling it slightly as you do, then sew firmly in place. Repeat with the other ear.

Insert a bit of stuffing into the muzzle to pad it out. Pin it to the front of the face and sew it in place. Using Color A, embroider a nose and mouth onto the muzzle. Using Color B, embroider a row of chain stitches around the neck opening and front band on the cardigan. Using Color C, embroider eyes and eyebrows onto the face, then embroider tiny buttons onto the front of the cardigan.

Reuben the Raccoon

Every neighborhood's little bandit is the raccoon, and ours calls for several color changes from his mask to his yellow polka-dot sweater to his black-and-gray striped tail. It's a perfect project to practice some techniques.

Height:

7" (17.8cm) measured from the tip of the ears to the base of the legs

Materials:

- DK weight (#3 light) yarn, approx. 1 oz (28.3g) in each shade:
  - **Color A** = White (1001)
  - **Color B** = Black (1002)
  - **Color C** = Hint of Silver (1807)
  - **Color D** = Buttermilk (1835)
  - **Color E** = Mustard (1823)
  - **Color F** = Meadow (1065)
- US size 6 (4mm) and US size 3 (3.25mm) knitting needles, or sizes required for gauge
- Blunt-end sewing needle
- Needlework scissors
- Stuffing
- 2 small black safety eyes (optional)

Gauge:

- 22 sts x 30 rows measure 4" x 4" (10.2 x 10.2cm) using US size 6 (4mm) needles and stockinette stitch.
- 24 sts x 36 rows measure 4" x 4" (10.2 x 10.2cm) using US size 3 (3.25mm needles and stockinette stitch.

Pattern Notes:

- The main piece of the raccoon is made in one piece. The ears, tail, and scarf are made separately.

BODY

Begin at the base of the legs.

Using Color B and US size 6 (4mm) needles, CO 34 sts.

Rows 1–4: Work in St st.

Break Color B and join Color C.

Rows 5–12: Work in St st.

Break Color C.

Sweater

Continuing from the body, join Color D.

Rows 1–4: Knit all stitches.

Begin pattern:

Rows 5–6: Work in St st.

Wind two small balls, one each of Colors D and E. Twist the yarns together when changing colors to ensure there are no holes in the work.

Row 7: *K3 D, k1 E*, rep from * to * to the last 2 sts, k2 D.

Row 8: Using D, purl all stitches.

Row 9: Using D, knit all stitches.

Row 10: P4 D, p1 E, *p3 D, p1 E*, rep from * to * to the last st, p1 D.

Row 11: Using D, knit all stitches.

Row 12: Using D, purl all stitches.

Row 13: *K3 D, k1 E*, rep from * to * to the last 2 sts, k2 D.

Break Color E and continue in Color D only.

Row 14: Purl all stitches.

Row 15: Knit all stitches.

Row 16: Purl all stitches.

Rows 17–18: Knit all stitches.

Break Color D.

Head

Continuing from the sweater, join Color A.

Rows 1–4: Work in St st.

Break Color A and join Color B.

Rows 5–8: Work in St st.

Break Color B and join Color A.

Rows 9–10: Work in St st.

Break Color A and join Color C.

Rows 11–12: Work in St st.

The next row starts shaping the head:

Row 13: *K2, k2tog*, rep from * to * to the last 2 sts, k2. (26 sts)

Row 14: Purl all stitches.

Row 15: *K1, k2tog*, rep from * to * to the last 2 sts, k2. (18 sts)

Row 16: Purl all stitches.

Row 17: K2tog to the end. (9 sts)

Row 18: Purl all stitches.

Break yarn and run through sts on the needle. Draw up tightly and bind off.

EARS (MAKE 2)

Using Color C and US size 3 (3.25mm) needles, CO 7 sts.

Rows 1–5: Knit all stitches.

Row 6: K2tog, k3, k2tog. (5 sts)

Row 7: Knit all stitches.

Break Color C and join Color B.

Row 8: K2tog, k1, k2tog. (3 sts)

Row 9: Knit all stitches.

Row 10: K3tog.

Bind off.

TAIL

Using Color C and US size 6 (4mm) needles, CO 10 sts.

Rows 1–4: Work in St st.

Break Color C and join Color B.

Rows 5–6: Work in St st.

Break Color B and join Color C.

Rows 7–8: Work in St st.

Break Color C and join Color B.

Rows 9–20: Rep Rows 5–8, continuing in stripe sequence.

Break Color C and join Color B.

Rows 21–22: Work in St st.

Bind off.

SCARF

Using Color F and US size 3 (3.25mm) needles, CO 5 sts.

Rows 1–28: (K1, p1) 2 times, k1.

Row 29: K2tog, k1, k2tog. (3 sts)

Rows 30–60: P1, k1, p1.

Row 61: Kfb, k1, kfb.

Rows 62–89: (K1, p1) 2 times, k1.

Bind off.

ASSEMBLING THE TOY

Follow the Step-by-Step Basic Toy instructions (page 27) for sewing the animal together, matching the colors and stripes as you do. Before stuffing, insert the safety eyes securely onto the face. Accentuate the eyes by sewing around one side of each eye with Color A. If not using safety eyes, embroider the eyes with Color B.

Stuff the toy quite firmly. Shape the head into a nice, rounded shape after gathering at the neckline. Embroider the nose and mouth with Color B. Sew the ears in place on either side of the head. Sew the tail into an oblong, matching the stripes. Secure it to the back of the animal. Work in the ends on the scarf and wrap it around the neck.

Lisbeth the Ladybug

The more little ladybugs the better, if you ask me—and gardeners will second that. These spotted friends act as a natural pest control.

I made my ladybug friend in traditional red and black, but orange- and yellow-spotted varieties would be equally sweet. You'll need your crochet hook to help finish up this toy.

Height:

7" (17.8cm) measured from the tip of the antennae to the base of the legs

Materials:

- DK weight (#3 light) yarn, approx. 1 oz (28.3g) in each shade:
  - **Color A** = Poppy (2170)
  - **Color B** = Toy (1844)
  - **Color C** = Black (1002)
- US size 6 (4mm) and US size 5 (3.75mm) knitting needles, or sizes required for gauge
- Blunt-end sewing needle
- Needlework scissors
- Stuffing
- Crochet hook

Gauge:

- 22 sts x 30 rows measure 4" x 4" (10.2 x 10.2cm) using US size 6 (4mm) needles and stockinette stitch.
- 23 sts x 32 rows measure 4" x 4" (10.2 x 10.2cm) using US size 5 (3.75mm) needles and stockinette stitch.

Pattern Notes:

- The main piece of the ladybug is made in one piece. The antennae, hood, and cape are made separately.

BODY

Begin at the base of the legs.

Using Color C and US size 6 (4mm) needles, CO 34 sts.

Rows 1–32: Work in St st.

Break Color C.

Head

Continuing from the body, join Color B.

Rows 1–12: Work in St st.

The next row starts shaping the head:

Row 13: *K2, k2tog*, rep from * to * to the last 2 sts, k2. (26 sts)

Row 14: Purl all stitches.

Row 15: *K1, k2tog*, rep from * to * to the last 2 sts, k2. (18 sts)

Row 16: Purl all stitches.

Row 17: K2tog to the end. (9 sts)

Row 18: Purl all stitches.

Break yarn and run through sts on the needle. Draw up tightly and bind off.

WINGS CAPE

Begin at the neck edge.

Using Color A and US size 5 (3.75mm) needles, CO 27 sts.

Rows 1–2: Knit all stitches.

Row 3 (hole row): K2, *yo, k2tog, k1*, rep from * to * to the last st, k1.

Rows 4–5: Knit all stitches.

Row 6: K7, m1, k13, m1, k7. (29 sts)

Row 7: K2, purl to the last 2 sts, k2.

Row 8: K7, m1, k1, m1, k13, m1, k1, m1, k7. (33 sts)

Row 9: K2, purl to the last 2 sts, k2.

Rows 10–13: Work in St st.

Row 14: (K13, kfb) 8 times, k13. (42 sts)

Row 15: K2, purl to the last 2 sts, k2.

Row 16: Knit all stitches.

Row 17: K2, purl to the last 2 sts, k2.

Divide for Wings

Row 18: K19, k2tog. Turn.

Row 19: K2, purl to the last 2 sts, k2.

Row 20: Knit all stitches.

Row 21: K2, purl to the last 2 sts, k2.

Row 22: K8, k2tog tbl, k2tog, k8. (18 sts)

Row 23: Rep Row 19.

Row 24: Knit all stitches.

Row 25: Rep Row 19.

Row 26: K2, k2tog tbl, k3, k2tog tbl, k2tog, k3, k2tog, k2. (14 sts)

Row 27: Rep Row 19.

Row 28: K2, k2tog tbl, k1, k2tog tbl, k2tog, k1, k2tog, k2. (10 sts)

Row 29: Rep Row 19.

Row 30: K2, sl1, k2tog, psso, k3tog, k2. (6 sts)

Row 31: K2, purl to the last 2 sts, k2.

Bind off.

Return to the remaining stitches and repeat to match the first wing.

CAPE TIE

Using Color A and US size 5 (3.75mm) needles, CO 3 sts.

Row 1: Sl1, k2.

Repeat Row 1 until the tie is approx. 15 ¾" (40cm).

Bind off.

CAPE HOOD

Using Color A and US size 5 (3.75mm) needles, CO 25 sts.

Rows 1–2: Knit all stitches.

Rows 3–7: Beg purl, work in St st.

The next row starts shaping the hood:

Row 8: *K3, k2tog*, rep from * to * to the end. (20 sts)

Row 9: Purl all stitches.

Row 10: *K2, k2tog*, rep from * to * to the end. (15 sts)

Row 11: Purl all stitches.

Row 12: *K1, k2tog*, rep from * to * to the end. (10 sts)

Row 13: Purl all stitches.

Row 14: K2tog to the end. (5 sts)

Break yarn and run through sts on the needle. Draw up and bind off.

ANTENNAE (MAKE 2)

Using Color C and US size 5 (3.75mm) needles, CO 20 sts.

Bind off.

ASSEMBLING THE TOY

Follow the Step-by-Step Basic Toy instructions (page 27) for sewing the animal together, stuffing quite firmly as you do. Shape the head into a nice, rounded shape after gathering at the neckline. Embroider the eyes and mouth using Color C. Make five small lengths of Color C and sew through the top of the face, just under where the hood will rest, for bangs. Secure each one with a few stitches.

Sew the seam on the cape hood. Use Color C to embroider spots in random places on the hood. Put the hood onto the head and hold it in place with a few stitches. Fold each end of the antennae over and secure with a few stitches to create the curly end. Using a large crochet hook, draw the other end of the antennae through the hood, leaving the curly end sticking out on either side. Stitch in place.

Use Color C to embroider spots in random places on the wings cape. Thread the cape tie through the holes at the neck edge. Place the cape onto the body and tie around the neck.

Oleander the Owl

Who knows what happens in the garden at night? Mr. Owl does. It's when he's just waking up. I love how the pretty purl stitch makes up his body.

Height:

7" (17.8cm) measured from the top of the head to the base of the feet

Materials:

- DK weight (#3 light) yarn, approx. 1 oz (28.3g) in each shade:
  - **Color A** = Dark Brown (1004)
  - **Color B** = Stone (1710)
  - **Color C** = Buttermilk (1835)
  - **Color D** = Black (1002)
  - **Color E** = Cream (1005)
- US size 6 (4mm) and US size 3 (3.25mm) knitting needles, or sizes required for gauge
- Blunt-end sewing needle
- Needlework scissors
- Stuffing

Gauge:

- 22 sts x 30 rows measure 4" x 4" (10.2 x 10.2cm) using US size 6 (4mm) needles and stockinette stitch.
- 24 sts x 36 rows measure 4" x 4" (10.2 x 10.2cm) using US size 3 (3.25mm) needles and stockinette stitch.

Pattern Notes:

- The main piece of the owl is made in one piece. The eye mask, beak, wings, and feet are made separately.

BODY

Begin at the base of the body.

Wind three small balls, two of Color A and one of Color B. Twist the yarns together when changing colors to ensure there are no holes in the work.

Using US size 6 (4mm) needles, CO 8 sts A, CO 18 sts B, CO 8 sts A.

Row 1: K8 A; using B, (k1, p1) 9 times; k8 A.

Row 2: P8 A, k18 B, p8 A.

Rows 3–32: Rep Rows 1–2.

Break Color B.

Head

Continuing from the body, work across all remaining stitches in Color A.

Rows 1–2: Knit all stitches.

Rows 3–14: Work in St st.

The next row starts shaping the head:

Row 15: *K2, k2tog*, rep from * to * to the last 2 sts, k2. (26 sts)

Row 16: Purl all stitches.

Row 17: *K1, k2tog*, rep from * to * to the last 2 sts, k2. (18 sts)

Row 18: Purl all stitches.

Row 19: K2tog to the end. (9 sts)

Row 20: Purl all stitches.

Break yarn and run through sts on the needle. Draw up tightly and bind off.

WINGS (MAKE 2)

Using Color A and US size 6 (4mm) needles, CO 3 sts.

Row 1: Knit all stitches.

Row 2: Kfb, k1, kfb. (5 sts)

Row 3: Knit all stitches.

Row 4: Kfb, k3, kfb. (7 sts)

Row 5: Knit all stitches.

Row 6: Kfb, k5, kfb. (9 sts)

Row 7: Knit all stitches.

Row 8: Kfb, k7, kfb. (11 sts)

Rows 9–17: Knit all stitches.

The next row starts shaping the top of the wing:

Row 18: K1, SKP, knit to the last 3 sts, k2tog, k1. (9 sts)

Row 19: Knit all stitches.

Row 20: K2tog to the last st, k1. (5 sts)

Bind off.

EYE MASK

Using Color E and US size 3 (3.25mm) needles, CO 4 sts.

Row 1: Purl all stitches.

Row 2: **Kfb, k2, kfb. (6 sts)

Row 3: Purl all stitches.

Row 4: Kfb, k4, kfb. (8 sts)

Row 5: Purl all stitches.

Row 6: K1, k2tog, k2, k2tog, k1. (6 sts)

Row 7: Purl all stitches.

Row 8: K1, k2tog, k2tog, k1. (4 sts)

Row 9: Purl all stitches.**

Rows 10–17: Rep from ** to **.

Bind off.

BEAK

Using Color C and US size 3 (3.25mm) needles, CO 2 sts.

Row 1: Knit all stitches.

Row 2: (Kfb) 2 times. (4 sts)

Row 3: Knit all stitches.

Row 4: Kfb, k2, kfb. (6 sts)

Row 5: Knit all stitches.

Row 6: Kfb, k4, kfb. (8 sts)

Row 7: Knit all stitches.

Bind off.

FEET

Using Color C and US size 3 (3.25mm) needles, CO 14 sts.

Rows 1–14: Work in St st.

Bind off.

ASSEMBLING THE TOY

Follow the Step-by-Step Basic Toy instructions (page 27) for sewing the animal together, stuffing quite firmly as you do. Do not sew the arms or legs on this toy. Attach the wings to either side of the body using the mattress stitch.

Pin the eye mask in place on the front of the head. Sew it in place, keeping a rounded shape as you do. Using Color B, work a row of chain stitches around each eye. Embroider sleepy eyes onto the mask using Color D. Fold the beak into a neat triangle, secure with a few stitches, and sew it to the face in the center of the mask. Sew the feet into a roll. Using Color A, sew around the feet to form the claws. Sew them onto the base of the body, curving them slightly as you do. Add some tufts of Color A to the top of the head on each side.

Piper the Puppy

Put our sweet puppy in a little one's hand, and they will carry their little friend everywhere. The stranding method gives his sweater a pretty pattern.

Height:

6 ½" (16.5cm) measured from the top of the head to the base of the legs

Materials:

- DK weight (#3 light) yarn, approx. 1 oz (28.3g) in each shade:
  - **Color A** = White (1001)
  - **Color B** = Parchment (1218)
  - **Color C** = Pistachio (1822)
  - **Color D** = Blush (1833)
  - **Color E** = Black (1002)
- US size 6 (4mm) and US size 3 (3.25mm) knitting needles, or sizes required for gauge
- Blunt-end sewing needle
- Needlework scissors
- Stuffing

Gauge:

- 22 sts x 30 rows measure 4" x 4" (10.2 x 10.2cm) using US size 6 (4mm) needles and stockinette stitch.
- 24 sts x 36 rows measure 4" x 4" (10.2 x 10.2cm) using US size 3 (3.25mm) needles and stockinette stitch.

Pattern Notes:

- The main piece of the puppy is made in one piece. The ears are made separately.

Dog Treats

BODY

Begin at the base of the legs.

Using Color A and US size 6 (4mm) needles, CO 34 sts.

Rows 1–6: Work in St st.

Break Color A and join Color B.

Rows 6–12: Work in St st.

Break Color B.

Sweater

Continuing from the body, join Color C.

Rows 1–2: Knit all stitches.

Rows 3–4: Work in St st.

Wind two small balls, one each of Colors C and D. Twist the yarns together when changing colors to ensure there are no holes in the work.

Begin pattern:

Row 5: *K1 C, k1 D*, rep from * to * to the end.

Row 6: *P1 C, p1 D*, rep from * to * to the end.

Rows 7–8: Rep Rows 5–6.

Rows 9–12: Using C, work in St st.

Rows 13–16: Rep Rows 5–6.

Rows 17–18: Using C, knit all stitches.

Break Colors C and D.

Head

Continue from the sweater. Wind two small balls, one each of Colors A and B. Twist the yarns together when changing colors to ensure there are no holes in the work.

Row 1: K11 B, k12 A, k11 B.

Row 2: P12 B, p10 A, p12 B.

Row 3: K13 B, k8 A, k13 B.

Row 4: P13 B, p8 A, p13 B.

Row 5: Rep Row 3.

Row 6: P14 B, p6 A, p14 B.

Row 7: K15 B, k4 A, k15 B.

Row 8: P15 B, p4 A, p15 B.

Row 9: K16 B, k2 A, k16 B.

Row 10: P16 B, p2 A, p16 B.

Rows 11–12: Rep Rows 9–10.

Break Color A and continue in Color B only.

The next row starts shaping the head:

Row 13: *K2, k2tog*, rep from * to * to the last 2 sts, k2. (26 sts)

Row 14: Purl all stitches.

Row 15: *K1, k2tog*, rep from * to * to the last 2 sts, k2. (18 sts)

Row 16: Purl all stitches.

Row 17: K2tog to the end. (9 sts)

Row 18: Purl all stitches.

Break yarn and run through sts on the needle. Draw up tightly and bind off.

EARS (MAKE 2)

Using Color B and US size 3 (3.25mm) needles, CO 3 sts.

Row 1: Knit all stitches.

Row 2: Kfb, k1, kfb. (5 sts)

Row 3: Knit all stitches.

Rows 4–5: Knit all stitches.

Row 6: K2tog, k1, k2tog. (3 sts)

Row 7: Knit all stitches.

Row 8: K3tog.

Bind off.

ASSEMBLING THE TOY

Follow the Step-by-Step Basic Toy instructions (page 27) for sewing the animal together, stuffing quite firmly as you do. Shape the head into a nice, rounded shape after gathering at the neckline. Using a blunt-end needle and Color A, continue the stripe on the head by working two duplicate stitches over four rows at the center front of the face. Embroider the eyes, nose, and mouth using Color E. Sew the ears horizontally onto either side of the head. Curl them under slightly.

Clementine the Cat

A kitty cat feels right at home among the wildflowers in the garden. Our little tabby can be a little tricky to complete, as it requires a few different balls of yarn at once, but he'll be dearly loved once he's finished.

Height:

7" (17.8cm) measured from the tip of the ears to the base of the legs

Materials:

- DK weight (#3 light) yarn, approx. 1 oz (28.3g) in each shade:
  - **Color A** = Parchment (1218)
  - **Color B** = Milky Tea (2172)
  - **Color C** = Vintage Peach (1836)
  - **Color D** = Candyfloss (1130)
  - **Color E** = White (1001)
- US size 6 (4mm) and US size 3 (3.25mm) knitting needles, or sizes required for gauge
- Blunt-end sewing needle
- Needlework scissors
- Stuffing

Gauge:

- 22 sts x 30 rows measure 4" x 4" (10.2 x 10.2cm) using US size 6 (4mm) needles and stockinette stitch.
- 24 sts x 36 rows measure 4" x 4" (10.2 x 10.2cm) using US size 3 (3.25mm) needles and stockinette stitch.

Special Abbreviations:

- **TW2F** = Worked over the next 2 sts as follows: Knit into the front of the second st but don't slip off the needle; knit into the first st in the usual way and slip both stitches off the needle at the same time.
- **TW2B** = Worked over the next 2 sts as follows: Knit into the back of the second st but do not slip off the needle; knit into the first st in the usual way and slip both stitches off the needle.

Pattern Notes:

- The main piece of the cat is made in one piece. The ears and tail are made separately.

BODY

Begin at the base of the legs.

Using Color E and US size 6 (4mm) needles, CO 34 sts.

Rows 1–4: Work in St st.

Break Color E and join Color A.

Begin stripes, breaking off and joining yarns as you work:

Row 5: Using A, knit all stitches.

Row 6: Using A, purl all stitches.

Row 7: Using B, knit all stitches.

Row 8: Using A, purl all stitches.

Row 9: Using A, knit all stitches.

Row 10: Using B, purl all stitches.

Row 11: Using A, knit all stitches.

Row 12: Using A, purl all stitches.

Break Colors A and B.

Sweater

Continuing from the body, join Color C.

Rows 1–5: Knit all stitches.

Begin pattern:

Row 6: P13, k2, p4, k2, p13.

Row 7: K15, TW2F, TW2B, k15.

Row 8: Rep Row 6.

Row 9: K15, TW2B, TW2F, k15.

Row 10: Rep Row 6.

Rows 11–22: Repeat Rows 7–10.

Rows 23–26: Knit all stitches.

Break Color C.

Head

Continue from the sweater.

Wind three small balls, one each of Colors A, B, and E. Twist the yarns together when changing colors to ensure there are no holes in the work. Break off and join yarns as you work:

Row 1: Using A, knit all stitches.

Row 2: Using A, purl all stitches.

Row 3: K13 A, k8 E, k13 A.

Row 4: P13 B, p8 E, p13 B.

Row 5: Rep Row 3.

Row 6: P14 A, p6 E, p14 A.

Row 7: K15 B, k4 E, k15 B.

Row 8: P16 A, p2 E, p16 A.

Break Colors B and E, and continue in Color A only.

Rows 9–12: Work in St st.

The next row starts shaping the head:

Row 13: *K2, k2tog*, rep from * to * to the last 2 sts, k2. (26 sts)

Row 14: Purl all stitches.

Row 15: *K1, k2tog*, rep from * to * to the last 2 sts, k2. (18 sts)

Row 16: Purl all stitches.

Row 17: K2tog to the end. (9 sts)

Row 18: Purl all stitches.

Break yarn and run through sts on the needle. Draw up tightly and bind off.

EARS (MAKE 2)

Using Color B and US size 3 (3.25mm) needles, CO 9 sts.

Rows 1–6: Knit all stitches.

Row 7: K2tog, k5, k2tog. (7 sts)

Row 8: Knit all stitches.

Row 9: K2tog, k3, k2tog. (5 sts)

Row 10: K2tog, k1, k2tog. (3 sts)

Row 11: K3tog.

Bind off.

TAIL

Using Color B and US size 3 (3.25mm) needles, CO 10 sts.

Rows 1–8: Work in St st.

Row 9: K3, (k2tog) 2 times, k3. (8 sts)

Row 10: Purl all stitches.

Rows 11–16: Work in St st.

Break Color B and join Color A.

Rows 17–20: Work in St st.

Row 21: K2tog, k4, k2tog. (6 sts)

Row 22: Purl all stitches.

Row 23: (K2tog) 3 times. (3 sts)

Row 24: P3tog.

Bind off.

ASSEMBLING THE TOY

Follow the Step-by-Step Basic Toy instructions (page 27) for sewing the animal together, matching the colors and stripes as you do. Using a blunt-end needle and Color B, work stripes of chain stitches onto the top section of the head in random areas. Sew an ear to either side of the head. Fold the tail in half lengthwise and sew the seam neatly with the mattress stitch. Sew to the back of the cat.

Embroider the eyes using Color B, and embroider the nose and mouth using Color D. Make three small lengths of Color B and sew through on either side of the nose for whiskers. Secure each one with a few stitches.

Fable the Fox

Our cool fox sports a turtleneck sweater made using a yarn chart. These cunning little fellows are drawn to yards as a safe and pretty place for their dens, just like your little ones will be drawn to these sweet little toys.

Height:

7" (17.8cm) measured from the tip of the ears to the base of the legs

Materials:

- DK weight (#3 light) yarn, approx. 1 oz (28.3g) in each shade:
  - **Color A** = Copper (1029)
  - **Color B** = Walnut (1054)
  - **Color C** = Cream (1005)
  - **Color D** = Black (1002)
  - **Color E** = Parchment (1218)
- US size 6 (4mm) and US size 3 (3.25mm) knitting needles, or sizes required for gauge
- Blunt-end sewing needle
- Needlework scissors
- Stuffing

Gauge:

- 22 sts x 30 rows measure 4" x 4" (10.2 x 10.2cm) using US size 6 (4mm) needles and stockinette stitch.
- 24 sts x 36 rows measure 4" x 4" (10.2 x 10.2cm) using US size 3 (3.25mm) needles and stockinette stitch.

Pattern Notes:

- The main piece of the fox is made in one piece. The ears, tail, and turtleneck collar are made separately.

FOX'S DEN
HEN HAVEN

BODY

Begin at the base of the legs.

Using Color D and US size 6 (4mm) needles, CO 34 sts.

Rows 1–4: Work in St st.

Break Color D and join Color A.

Rows 5–12: Work in St st.

Break Color A.

Sweater

Continuing from the body, join Color E.

Rows 1–4: Knit all stitches.

Rows 5–6: Work in St st.

Wind two small balls, one each of Colors B and E. When working from the chart, strand the yarn loosely across the back of the work.

Rows 7–8: Work in St st.

Rows 9–17: Follow the Fox Pattern Chart. Read rows from right to left.

Break Color B and continue in Color E only.

Rows 18–20: Beg purl, work in St st.

Rows 21–24: Knit all stitches.

Break Color E.

Key:

X = Color B

Fox Pattern Chart

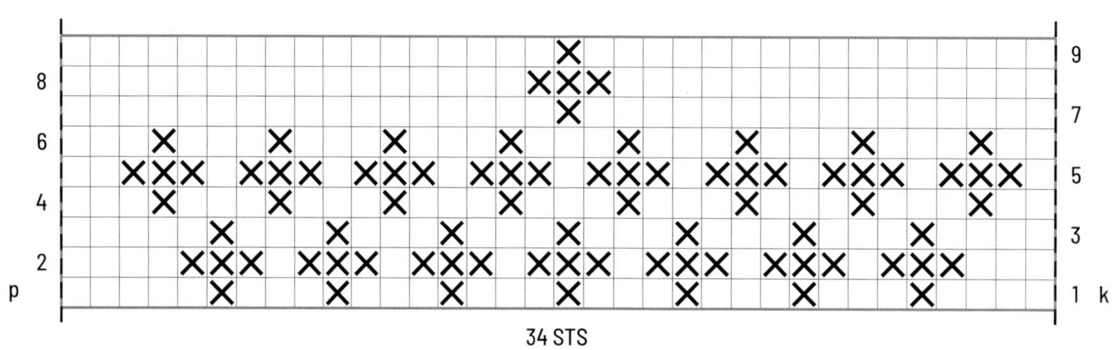

Head

Continuing from the sweater, join Color C.

Rows 1–4: Work in St st.

Wind two small balls, one each of Colors A and C. Twist the yarns together when changing colors to ensure there are no holes in the work.

Row 5: K16 C, k2 A, k16 C.

Row 6: P12 C, p10 A, p12 C.

Row 7: K10 C, k14 A, k10 C.

Row 8: P9 C, p16 A, p9 C.

Break Color C and continue in Color A only.

Rows 9–12: Work in St st.

The next row starts shaping the head:

Row 13: *K2, k2tog*, rep from * to * to the last 2 sts, k2. (26 sts)

Row 14: Purl all stitches.

Row 15: *K1, k2tog*, rep from * to * to the last 2 sts, k2. (18 sts)

Row 16: Purl all stitches.

Row 17: K2tog to the end. (9 sts)

Row 18: Purl all stitches.

Break yarn and run through sts on the needle. Draw up tightly and bind off.

EARS (MAKE 2)

Using Color A and US size 3 (3.25mm) needles, CO 7 sts.

Rows 1–6: Work in St st.

Row 7: K2tog, k3, k2tog. (5 sts)

Row 8: Knit all stitches.

Break Color A and join Color D.

Row 9: K2tog, k1, k2tog. (3 sts)

Row 10: Knit all stitches.

Row 11: K3tog.

Bind off.

TAIL

Using Color A and US size 6 (4mm) needles, CO 16 sts.

Rows 1–4: Work in St st.

Row 5: (K2, k2tog) 4 times. (12 sts)

Row 6: Purl all stitches.

Rows 7–10: Work in St st.

Row 11: (K1, k2tog) 4 times. (8 sts)

Row 12: Purl all stitches.

Rows 13–16: Work in St st.

Break Color A and join Color D.

Rows 17–18: Work in St st.

Row 19: (K2, k2tog) 2 times. (6 sts)

Row 20: Purl all stitches.

Row 21: (K2tog) 3 times. (3 sts)

Row 22: K3tog.

Bind off.

COLLAR

Using Color E and US size 6 (4mm) needles, CO 28 sts.

Rows 1–3: *K1, p1*, rep from * to * to the end.

Bind off in pattern.

ASSEMBLING THE TOY

Follow the Step-by-Step Basic Toy instructions (page 27) for sewing the animal together, stuffing quite firmly as you do. Shape the head into a nice, rounded shape after gathering at the neckline. Using a blunt-end needle and Color A, form part of the nose by working two duplicate stitches over one row at the center front of the face. Embroider the eyes and nose using Color D. Place the collar around the neck and join the short ends. Stitch it in place onto the body to secure. Sew the ears in place on either side of the head. Secure the tail to the back of the animal.

Wendell the Weasel

Boy, does our weasel pop in his fancy sweater, bow tie, and flatcap! The two-color patterning is worked from a chart using the stranding method while duplicate stitches are used to work his nose.

Height:

7" (17.8cm) measured from the top of the hat to the base of the legs

Materials:

- DK weight (#3 light) yarn, approx. 1 oz (28.3g) in each shade:

  Color A = Copper (1029)

  Color B = Cream (1005)

  Color C = Black (1002)

  Color D = Lincoln (1834)

  Color E = Wisteria (1432)

  Color F = Merlot (2090)

  Color G = Gorse Nepp (Life DK 2337)
- US size 6 (4mm) and US size 3 (3.25mm) knitting needles, or sizes required for gauge
- Blunt-end sewing needle
- Needlework scissors
- Stuffing

Gauge:

- 22 sts x 30 rows measure 4" x 4" (10.2 x 10.2cm) using US size 6 (4mm) needles and stockinette stitch.
- 24 sts x 36 rows measure 4" x 4" (10.2 x 10.2cm) using US size 3 (3.25mm) needles and stockinette stitch.

Pattern Notes:

- The main piece of the weasel is made in one piece. The ears, tail, bow tie, and hat are made separately.

MISSING

BODY

Begin at the base of the legs.

Using Color C and US size 6 (4mm) needles, CO 34 sts.

Row 1: Knit all stitches.

Row 2: Purl all stitches.

Break Color C and join Color A.

Rows 3–12: Work in St st.

Break Color A.

Sweater

Continuing from the body, join Color D.

Rows 1–2: Knit all stitches.

Wind two small balls, one each of Colors D and E. When working from the chart, strand the yarn loosely across the back of the work.

Rows 3–17: Follow the Weasel Pattern Chart. Read rows from right to left.

Break Color E and continue in Color D only.

Row 18: Purl all stitches.

Rows 19–20: Knit all stitches.

Break Color D.

Head

Continue from the sweater.

Wind three small balls, two of Color A and one of Color B. Twist the yarns together when changing colors to ensure there are no holes in the work.

Row 1: K14 A, k6 B, k14 A.

Key:

X = Color E

Weasel Pattern Chart

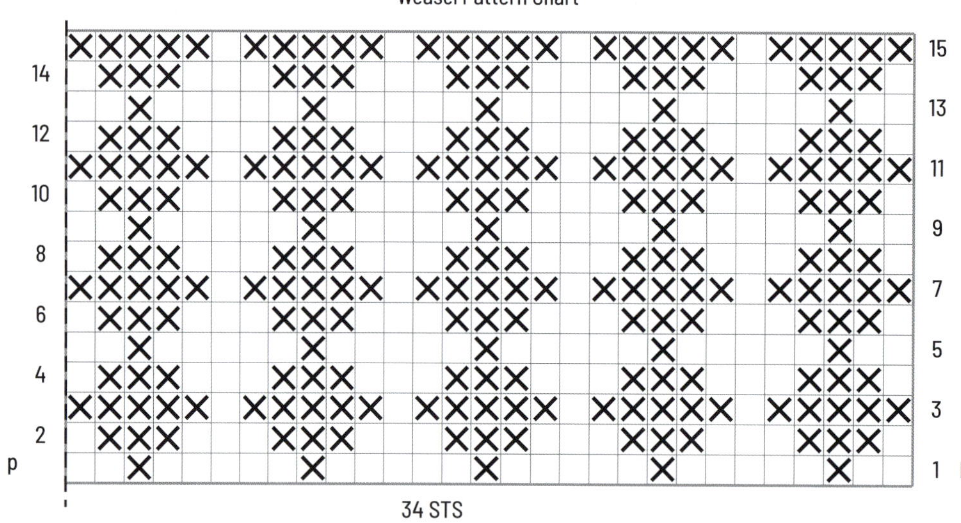

Row 2: P12 A, p10 B, p12 A.

Row 3: K10 A, k14 B, k10 A.

Row 4: P9 A, p16 B, p9 A

Row 5: K7 A, k20 B, k7 A.

Row 6: P8 A, p18 B, p8 A.

Break Color B and continue in Color A only.

Rows 7–12: Work in St st.

The next row starts shaping the head:

Row 13: *K2, k2tog*, rep from * to * to the last 2 sts, k2. (26 sts)

Row 14: Purl all stitches.

Row 15: *K1, k2tog*, rep from * to * to the last 2 sts, k2. (18 sts)

Row 16: Purl all stitches.

Row 17: K2tog to the end. (9 sts)

Row 18: Purl all stitches.

Break yarn and run through sts on the needle. Draw up tightly and bind off.

EARS (MAKE 2)

Using Color A and US size 3 (3.25mm) needles, CO 4 sts.

Row 1: Knit all stitches.

Row 2: Kfb to the end. (8 sts)

Rows 3–6: Knit all stitches.

Row 7: (K2tog) 4 times. (4 sts)

Bind off.

TAIL

Using Color A and US size 3 (3.25mm) needles, CO 5 sts.

Rows 1–22: Work in St st.

Break Color A and join Color C.

Rows 23–24: Work in St st.

Row 25: K2tog, k1, k2tog. (3 sts)

Row 26: P3tog.

Bind off.

BOW TIE

Using Color F and US size 3 (3.25mm) needles, CO 5 sts.

Rows 1–14: Knit all stitches.

Bind off.

FLATCAP

Using Color G and US size 3 (3.25mm) needles, CO 6 sts.

Row 1: Kfb to the end. (12 sts)

Row 2: Knit all stitches.

Row 3: Kfb to the end. (24 sts)

Row 4: Knit all stitches.

Rows 5–10: Work in St st.

Bind off.

BRIM

Using Color G and US size 3 (3.25mm) needles, CO 34 sts.

Rows 1–4: Knit all stitches.

Bind off.

ASSEMBLING THE TOY

Follow the Step-by-Step Basic Toy instructions (page 27) for sewing the animal together, stuffing quite firmly as you do. Shape the head into a nice, rounded shape after gathering at the neckline. Using a blunt-end needle and Color A, form part of the nose by working four duplicate stitches over two rows at the center front of the face. Embroider the eyes, eyebrows, and nose using Color C. Make three small lengths of Color C and sew through on either side of the nose for whiskers. Secure each one with a few stitches.

Sew an ear to either side of the head. Fold the tail in half lengthwise and sew the seam neatly. Stitch it to the back of the weasel. Gather the center of the bow tie to form a bow shape. Sew it to the front of the body. Sew the seam on the hat with the mattress stitch. Gather the outer edge of the piece to form the crown. Join the brim into a circle and attach it to the top of the hat; pull it into a V shape at the front to form a tiny peak. Secure it to the head with a few stitches.

Baxter the Badger

Our little country badger is dressed for gardening in his overalls and spotted red bandana. The patch on his knee is such a sweet touch. He'll quickly win over your little ones.

Height:

7" (17.8cm) measured from the tip of the ears to the base of the legs

Materials:

- DK weight (#3 light) yarn, approx. 1 oz (28.3g) in each shade:
  - **Color A** = Black (1002)
  - **Color B** = White (1001)
  - **Color C** = Lipstick (1246)
  - **Color D** = Denim (1302)
  - **Color E** = Storm Blue (1722)
  - **Color F** = Gray (1099)
- US size 6 (4mm) and US size 3 (3.25mm) knitting needles, or sizes required for gauge
- Blunt-end sewing needle
- Needlework scissors
- Stuffing

Gauge:

- 22 sts x 30 rows measure 4" x 4" (10.2 x 10.2cm) using US size 6 (4mm) needles and stockinette stitch.
- 24 sts x 36 rows measure 4" x 4" (10.2 x 10.2cm) using US size 3 (3.25mm) needles and stockinette stitch.

Pattern Notes:

- The main piece of the badger is made in one piece. The bandana and patch are made separately. The overalls bib is separate from the body but continued from a row in the pants.
- This animal is slightly different, as the ears are defined by sewing through the head on either side. Because of this, no decreases are used to shape the head.

BODY

Begin at the base of the legs.

Using Color F and US size 6 (4mm) needles, CO 34 sts.

Rows 1–8: Work in St st.

Break Color F.

Overalls Pants

Continuing from the body, join Color D.

Rows 1–2: Knit all stitches.

Rows 3–11: Work in St st.

Row 12: Knit all stitches. Mark this row.

Break Color D.

Torso

Continuing from the overalls pants, join Color F.

Rows 13–24: Work in St st.

Break Color F.

Head

Continuing from the torso, join Color B.

Rows 1–6: Work in St st.

Wind two small balls, one each of Colors A and B. When working from the chart, strand the yarn loosely across the back of the work.

Rows 7–16: Follow the Badger Pattern Chart. Read rows from right to left.

Bind off.

Key:

X = Color A

Badger Pattern Chart

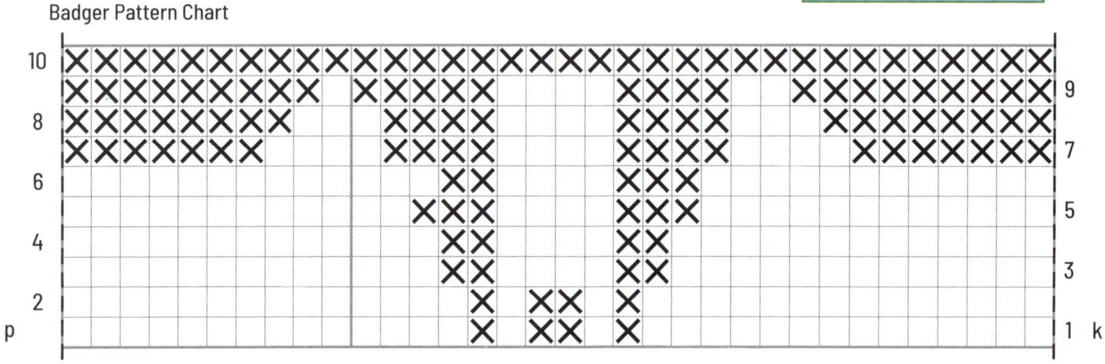

34 STS

OVERALLS BIB

Count 13 sts in from the right-hand side of the work on the marked Row 12 and join Color D. With the right side of the work facing, pick up and knit the next 8 sts. Turn and work on these sts for the bib.

Row 1: K1, purl to the last st, k1.

Row 2: Knit all stitches.

Rows 3–6: Rep Rows 1–2.

Rows 7–8: Knit all stitches.

Bind off.

OVERALLS STRAPS (MAKE 2)

Using Color D and US size 3 (3.25mm) needles, CO 20 sts.

Bind off.

BANDANA

Using Color C and US size 3 (3.25mm) needles, CO 3 sts.

Row 1: Knit all stitches.

Row 2: Kfb, k1, kfb. (5 sts)

Row 3: K2, p1, k2.

Row 4: K1, kfb, k1, kfb, k1. (7 sts)

Row 5: K2, p3, k2.

Row 6: K1, kfb, k3, kfb, k1. (9 sts)

Row 7: K2, p5, k2.

Row 8: K1, kfb, k5, kfb, k1. (11 sts)

Row 9: K2, p7, k2.

Row 10: K1, kfb, k7, kfb, k1. (13 sts)

Row 11: K2, p9, k2.

Row 12: K1, kfb, k9, kfb, k1. (15 sts)

Row 13: K2, p11, k2.

Row 14: Knit all stitches.

Bind off.

BANDANA TIES (MAKE 2)

Using Color C and US size 3 (3.25mm) needles, CO 33 sts.

Bind off.

PATCH

Using Color E and US size 3 (3.25mm) needles, CO 5 sts.

Rows 1–5: Knit all stitches.

Bind off.

ASSEMBLING THE TOY

This toy is sewn up a little bit differently from to the basic toy; instead of gathering the top, sew the seam that runs down the center back of the toy, then sew the top of the head horizontally. Stuff and shape the head following the Step-by-Step Basic Toy instructions (page 27). To define the ears, sew diagonally through both thicknesses of the head on either side at the top. Embroider the eyes using Color A.

Sew the overall straps on either side of the bib. Cross the straps at the back of the toy and stitch them to the waistline of the pants. Stitch the patch onto one leg using Color A. Sew the bandana ties to each side of the bandana. Embroider white dots onto the bandana in random places using Color B. Wrap the bandana around the neck and tie at the back.

Scarlett the Skunk

There's nothing stinky about our little skunk. She's as sweet as can be with her coif and tail trimmed in eyelash yarn and a pink heart motif embellishing her belly.

Height:

7 ½" (19.1cm) measured from the tip of the bow to the base of the legs

Materials:

- DK weight (#3 light) yarn, approx. 1 oz (28.3g) in each shade:
  - **Color A** = Black (1002)
  - **Color B** = White (1001)
  - **Color C** = Fondant (1241)
- Eyelash yarn, approx. 1 oz (28.3g) in each shade:
  - **Color D** = Black (474)
  - **Color E** = White (470)
- US size 6 (4mm) and US size 3 (3.25mm) knitting needles, or sizes required for gauge
- Blunt-end sewing needle
- Needlework scissors
- Stuffing
- 2 small black safety eyes (optional)

Gauge:

- **DK-weight yarn:** 22 sts x 30 rows measure 4" x 4" (10.2 x 10.2cm) using US size 6 (4mm) needles and stockinette stitch.
- **DK-weight yarn:** 24 sts x 36 rows measure 4" x 4" (10.2 x 10.2cm) using US size 3 (3.25mm) needles and stockinette stitch.
- **Eyelash yarn:** 22 sts x 28 rows measure 4" x 4" (10.2 x 10.2cm) using US size 6 (4mm) needles and stockinette stitch.

Pattern Notes:

- The main piece of the skunk is made in one piece. The bow, ears, muzzle, back cover, and tail are made separately.

BODY

Begin at the base of the legs.

Using Color A and US size 6 (4mm) needles, CO 34 sts.

Rows 1–12: Work in St st.

Break Color A and join Color B.

Rows 13–32: Work in St st.

Break Color B.

Head

Continuing from the body, join Color A.

Rows 1–12: Work in St st.

The next row starts shaping the head:

Row 13: *K2, k2tog*, rep from * to * to the last 2 sts, k2. (26 sts)

Row 14: Purl all stitches.

Row 15: *K1, k2tog*, rep from * to * to the last 2 sts, k2. (18 sts)

Row 16: Purl all stitches.

Row 17: K2tog to the end. (9 sts)

Row 18: Purl all stitches.

Break yarn and run through sts on the needle. Draw up tightly and bind off.

EARS (MAKE 2)

Using Color A and US size 3 (3.25mm) needles, CO 4 sts.

Row 1: Knit all stitches.

Row 2: Kfb to the end. (8 sts)

Rows 3–6: Knit all stitches.

Row 7: (K2tog) 4 times. (4 sts)

Bind off.

MUZZLE

Using Color A and US size 3 (3.25mm) needles, CO 3 sts.

Row 1: Purl all stitches.

Row 2: Kfb, k1, kfb. (5 sts)

Row 3: Purl all stitches.

Row 4: Kfb, k3, kfb. (7 sts)

Row 5: Purl all stitches.

Row 6: K2tog, k3, k2tog. (5 sts)

Row 7: Purl all stitches.

Row 8: K2tog, k1, k2tog. (3 sts)

Row 9: Purl all stitches.

Bind off.

BACK COVER

Tip

Counting rows when using eyelash yarns isn't easy, so mark them down as you work.

Using Color E and US size 6 (4mm) needles, CO 3 sts.

Rows 1–6: Work in St st.

Row 7: Kfb, k1, kfb. (5 sts)

Row 8: Purl all stitches.

Row 9: Kfb, k3, kfb. (7 sts)

Row 10: Purl all stitches.

Row 11: CO 3 sts, knit all stitches. (10 sts)

Row 12: CO 3 sts, purl all stitches. (13 sts)

Row 13: Kfb, knit to last st, kfb. (15 sts)

Row 14: Purl all stitches.

Row 15: CO 2 sts, knit all stitches. (17 sts)

Row 16: CO 2 sts, purl all stitches. (19 sts)

Row 17: Knit all stitches.

Row 18: Purl all stitches.

Row 19: Kfb, knit to last st, kfb. (21 sts)

Row 20: Purl all stitches.

Row 21: Kfb, knit to last st, kfb. (23 sts)

Row 22: Purl all stitches.

Rows 23–32: Work in St st.

Wind two small balls, one each of Colors D and E. Strand the yarn loosely across the back of the work.

Row 33: K8 E, k7 D, k8 E.

Row 34: P8 E, p7 D, p8 E.

Repeat Rows 33–34 for a further 4" (10.2cm), ending on a Row 34.

Bind off.

TAIL

Wind three small balls, two of Color E and one of Color D. Twist the yarns together when changing colors to ensure there are no holes in the work.

Using US size 6 (4mm) needles, CO 8 sts E, CO 20 sts D, CO 8 sts E.

Row 1: K8 E, k20 D, k8 E.

Row 2: P8 E, p20 D, p8 E.

Repeat Rows 1–2 until the piece measures 4 ¾" (12.1cm), ending on a Row 2.

Next Row: K2tog 8 E, k2tog 20 D, k2tog 8 E. (18 sts)

Next Row: P2tog 4 E, p2tog 10 D, p2tog 4 E. (9 sts)

Break yarns and thread one piece of yarn through the remaining sts on the needle. Draw up and bind off.

BOW

Using Color C and US size 3 (3.25mm) needles, CO 6 sts.

Rows 1–20: Knit all stitches.

Bind off.

ASSEMBLING THE TOY

Follow the Step-by-Step Basic Toy instructions (page 27) for sewing the animal together, matching the colors as you do. Before stuffing, insert the safety eyes securely onto the face. Accentuate the eyes by sewing around one side of each eye with Color B. If not using safety eyes, embroider the eyes with Color B.

Using a blunt-end needle and Color C, form a heart on the belly by working duplicate stitches over seven rows, starting at Row 18 of the body. Follow the Skunk Pattern Chart. Read rows from right to left.

Stuff the toy quite firmly. Shape the head into a nice, rounded shape after gathering at the neckline. Gather the muzzle around the outer edge and form it into a cup shape. Add a small amount of stuffing and sew it in place into the front of the head. Embroider the nose and mouth with Color C.

Sew the back cover onto the body, shaping it around the neck and body. Sew the seam on the tail, which runs down the back of the piece, and stitch it to the base of the body. Sew the ears in place on either side of the head and back cover. Gather the center of the bow to give it a nice shape. Sew the bow to the top of the head.

Key:

X = Color C

Skunk Pattern Chart

Row						Row
	X				X	7
6	X	X		X	X	
	X	X	X	X	X	5
4	X	X	X	X	X	
	X	X	X	X	X	3
2		X	X	X		
p			X			1 k

5 STS

Marcel the Mouse

What garden is complete without a mischief of mice? Once you finish your first one, you'll be eager to start the next. Pick a different sweater color for each little critter in your nest.

Height:

7" (17.8cm) measured from the tip of the ears to the base of the legs

Materials:

- DK weight (#3 light) yarn, approx. 1 oz (28.3g) in each shade:
  - **Color A** = Warm Grey (1805)
  - **Color B** = Black (1002)
  - **Color C** = Candyfloss (1130)
  - **Color D** = White (1001)
  - **Color E** = Amber (King Cole 3323)
- US size 6 (4mm) and US size 3 (3.25mm) knitting needles, or sizes required for gauge
- Blunt-end sewing needle
- Needlework scissors
- Stuffing

Gauge:

- 22 sts x 30 rows measure 4" x 4" (10.2 x 10.2cm) using US size 6 (4mm) needles and stockinette stitch.
- 24 sts x 36 rows measure 4" x 4" (10.2 x 10.2cm) using US size 3 (3.25mm) needles and stockinette stitch.

Special Abbreviations:

- **TW2F** = Worked over the next 2 sts as follows: Knit into the front of the second st but don't slip off the needle; knit into the first st in the usual way and slip both stitches off the needle at the same time.
- **TW2B** = Worked over the next 2 sts as follows: Knit into the back of the second st but do not slip off the needle; knit into the first st in the usual way and slip both stitches off the needle.

Pattern Notes:

- The main piece of the mouse is made in one piece. The ears and tail are made separately.

Knitty Gritty
Cheese
CHEESE SAMPLES
- CHEDDAR
- GOUDA
- NOT SO GOUDA
- BRIE
- GRUYERE
- PARMESAN

BODY

Begin at the base of the legs.

Using Color A and US size 6 (4mm) needles, CO 34 sts.

Rows 1–12: Work in St st.

Break Color A.

Sweater

Continuing from the body, join Color E.

Begin pattern:

Rows 1–2: Knit all stitches.

Row 3: K8, (p2, TW2F) 4 times, p2, k8.

Row 4: P8, (k2, p2) 4 times, k2, p8.

Row 5: K8, (p2, TW2B) 4 times, p2, k8.

Row 6: Rep Row 4.

Rows 7–18: Rep Rows 3–6.

Rows 19–20: Knit all stitches.

Break Color E.

Head

Continue from the sweater.

Wind three small balls, two of Color A and one of Color D. Twist the yarns together when changing colors to ensure there are no holes in the work.

Row 1: K14 A, k6 D, k14 A.

Row 2: P12 A, p10 D, p12 A.

Row 3: K10 A, k14 D, k10 A.

Row 4: P10 A, p14 D, p10 A.

Break Color D and continue in Color A only.

Rows 5–12: Work in St st.

The next row starts shaping the head:

Row 13: *K2, k2tog*, rep from * to * to the last 2 sts, k2. (26 sts)

Row 14: Purl all stitches.

Row 15: *K1, k2tog*, rep from * to * to the last 2 sts, k2. (18 sts)

Row 16: Purl all stitches.

Row 17: K2tog to the end. (9 sts)

Row 18: Purl all stitches.

Break yarn and run through sts on the needle. Draw up tightly and bind off.

OUTER EARS (MAKE 2)

Using Color A and US size 3 (3.25mm) needles, CO 6 sts.

Row 1: Purl all stitches.

Row 2: Kfb to the end. (12 sts)

Row 3: K1, purl to the last st, k1.

Row 4: Knit all stitches.

Rows 5–8: Rep Rows 3–4.

Row 9: (K2tog) 6 times. (6 sts)

Bind off.

INNER EARS (MAKE 2)

Using Color C and US size 3 (3.25mm) needles, CO 4 sts.

Row 1: Purl all stitches.

Row 2: Kfb to the end. (8 sts)

Row 3: K1, purl to the last st, k1.

Row 4: Knit all stitches.

Rows 5–6: Rep Rows 3–4.

Row 7: (K2tog) 4 times. (4 sts)

Bind off.

TAIL

Using Color C and US size 3 (3.25mm) needles, CO 6 sts.

Rows 1–18: Work in St st.

Row 19: K2tog, k2, k2tog. (4 sts)

Row 20: Purl all stitches.

Row 21: Knit all stitches.

Row 22: (P2tog) 2 times. (2 sts)

Row 23: K2tog.

Bind off.

ASSEMBLING THE TOY

Follow the Step-by-Step Basic Toy instructions (page 27) for sewing the animal together, stuffing quite firmly as you do. Shape the head into a nice, rounded shape after gathering at the neckline. Using a blunt-end needle and Color A, form part of the nose by working four duplicate stitches over two rows at the center front of the face. Embroider the eyes and eyebrows using Color B, and embroider the nose using Color C. Make three small lengths of Color A and sew through on either side of the nose for whiskers. Secure each one with a few stitches.

Run Color A or C (depending on whether you're working on the outer or inner ear) all around the outer edge of the ear and draw up slightly to give a neat curve. Repeat on the remaining ear pieces. Place the inner ears inside the outer ears and stitch in place. Sew an ear to either side of the head. Fold the tail in half lengthwise and sew the seam neatly. Stitch it to the back of the mouse.

Sage the Squirrel

This fancy squirrel calls for a collection of different yarn colors and textures, making him super fun to complete. The ears and tail use eyelash yarn that is knitted separately and sewn on afterward.

Height:

7" (17.8cm) measured from the tip of the ears to the base of the legs

Materials:

- DK weight (#3 light) yarn, approx. 1 oz (28.3g) in each shade:
  - **Color A** = Copper (1029)
  - **Color B** = Sherbert (1034)
  - **Color C** = Cream (1005)
  - **Color D** = Black (1002)
  - **Color E** = Denim (1302)
  - **Color F** = Storm Blue (1722)
- Eyelash yarn, approx. 1 oz (28.3g) in each shade:
  - **Color G** = Ginger (1876)
- US size 6 (4mm) and US size 3 (3.25mm) knitting needles, or sizes required for gauge
- Blunt-end sewing needle
- Needlework scissors
- Stuffing

Gauge:

- **DK-weight yarn:** 22 sts x 30 rows measure 4" x 4" (10.2 x 10.2cm) using US size 6 (4mm) needles and stockinette stitch.
- **DK-weight yarn:** 24 sts x 36 rows measure 4" x 4" (10.2 x 10.2cm) using US size 3 (3.25mm) needles and stockinette stitch.
- **Eyelash yarn:** 22 sts x 28 rows measure 4" x 4" (10.2 x 10.2cm) using US size 6 (4mm) needles and stockinette stitch.

Pattern Notes:

- The main piece of the squirrel is made in one piece. The ears, tail, apron, and apron pocket are made separately.

Special Safety Note

The tiny paintbrushes shown are for display purposes only to enhance the photograph and would be a safety hazard for little ones.

PAINT
PAINT COLOUR
ALL PURPOSE PAINT

BODY

Begin at the base of the legs.

Using Color A and US size 6 (4mm) needles, CO 34 sts.

Rows 1–12: Work in St st.

Break Color A.

Sweater

Continue from the body.

Wind two small balls, one each of Colors B and C. Carry the yarn up the side of the work while knitting the stripes.

Rows 1–2: Using B, knit all stitches.

Rows 3–4: Using B, work in St st.

Rows 5–6: Using C, work in St st.

Rows 7–8: Using B, work in St st.

Rows 9–16: Rep Rows 5–8.

Rows 17–18: Using B, knit all stitches.

Break Colors B and C.

Head

Continue from the sweater.

Wind three small balls, two of Color A and one of Color C. Twist the yarns together when changing colors to ensure there are no holes in the work.

Row 1: K14 A, k6 C, k14 A.

Row 2: P12 A, p10 C, p12 A.

Row 3: K10 A, k14 C, k10 A.

Row 4: P9 A, p16 C, p9 A.

Row 5: K7 A, k20 C, k7 A.

Row 6: P8 A, p18 C, p8 A.

Break Color C and continue in Color A only.

Rows 7–12: Work in St st.

The next row starts shaping the head:

Row 13: *K2, k2tog*, rep from * to * to the last 2 sts, k2. (26 sts)

Row 14: Purl all stitches.

Row 15: *K1, k2tog*, rep from * to * to the last 2 sts, k2. (18 sts)

Row 16: Purl all stitches.

Row 17: K2tog to the end. (9 sts)

Row 18: Purl all stitches.

Break yarn and run through sts on the needle. Draw up tightly and bind off.

EARS (MAKE 2)

Using Color A and US size 3 (3.25mm) needles, CO 7 sts.

Rows 1–6: Work in St st.

Row 7: K2tog, k3, k2tog. (5 sts)

Row 8: Knit all stitches.

Row 9: K2tog, k1, k2tog. (3 sts)

Row 10: Knit all stitches.

Row 11: K3tog.

Bind off.

TAIL

Using Color G and US size 6 (4mm) needles, CO 24 sts.

Rows 1–10: Work in St st.

Row 11: (K2, k2tog) 6 times. (18 sts)

Row 12: Purl all stitches.

Rows 13–18: Work in St st.

Row 19: (K1, k2tog) 6 times. (12 sts)

Row 20: Purl all stitches.

Rows 21–24: Work in St st.

Row 25: (K2tog) 6 times. (6 sts)

Row 26: Purl all stitches.

Row 27: (K2tog) 3 times. (3 sts)

Row 28: P3tog.

Bind off.

APRON

Using Color E and US size 3 (3.25mm) needles, CO 18 sts.

Rows 1–2: Knit all stitches.

Rows 3–10: Work in St st.

Row 11: CO 22 sts, knit across cast-on sts, knit across sts on the needle.

Row 12: CO 22 sts, knit across cast-on sts, knit across sts on the needle. (62 sts)

Row 13: Knit all stitches.

Bind off.

APRON POCKET

Using Color F and US size 3 (3.25mm) needles, CO 7 sts.

Rows 1–7: *K1, p1*, rep from * to * to the last st, k1.

Bind off in pattern.

ASSEMBLING THE TOY

Follow the Step-by-Step Basic Toy instructions (page 27) for sewing the animal together, stuffing quite firmly as you do. Shape the head into a nice, rounded shape after gathering at the neckline. Using a blunt-end needle and Color A, form part of the nose by working seven duplicate stitches over three rows at the center front of the face. Embroider the eyes and nose using Color D.

Stitch an ear to either side of the head, sewing a few strands of Color G onto the tip of each ear. Fold the tail in half, the seam running down the center back. Stitch the seam, gather the base slightly, and sew the tail to the back of the toy. Sew the pocket onto the front of the apron, leaving the top section open. Tie the aprong around the waist of the toy.

Index

About the Author

Val Pierce's passion for knitting began when her father taught her to knit at the age of five. Later in life, she began home knitting for yarn manufacturers, and since then, she has made a huge range of items, from evening dresses to teddy bears. She later began designing items of her own, and before long, Val's designs were appearing regularly in national knitting and crochet magazines. She has written numerous best-selling knitting and crochet books, which include *One-Stitch Baby Knits, Cutest Ever Baby Knits, Cutest Ever Toddler Knits, Knitting for Winter, Love . . . Knitting*, and *Learn to Knit the Easy Way*. She also teaches knitting and crochet, as well as a range of other needlecrafts, to both adults and children. Val lives and works in Shropshire. See more at her website, www.crossedneedles.co.uk.

Acknowledgments

Firstly, I would like to thank Fox Chapel Publishing for giving me the opportunity to write this lovely book. Thanks as always, go to the wonderful team of editors, technical editors, and designers without whose help and expertise this publication would not have been possible.

I would also like to express my gratitude to the yarn companies who sponsored me; in particular, Stylecraft Yarns who supplied me with their beautiful yarns to create most of the projects in the book.

Many thanks to Steve Watts (A Decent Exposure Photography, www.adecentexposure.co.uk) for his brilliant photography and Ben Walton, set designer (BA Hons Model Making), for his intricate and fantastic models that were used to enhance the photography.

A big thank-you to my very cute models William and Neeve Cotterill, who were a joy to work with.

Last but by no means least, many thanks to all my family and friends for their support and encouragement while writing this book.